The Coming Crash Can Be Prevented

Americans Must Know
What Macron Has Done

Jan. 9—French President Emmanuel Macron, in his speech in Xi'an on the first leg of his visit to China, has unleashed a highly significant intervention into the nearly universal idiocy dominating the European Union.

To make a transformation of this sort requires, first, the acknowledgment of the horror now dominating the political and economic conditions in the West, and the degenerate frame of mind of the elites, the media, and much of the population in Europe and the United States.

Secondly, it requires acknowledgment of the historic New Paradigm unleashed by China's New Silk Road.

Third, it requires the vision to see that bringing Europe and the United States to fully join with China's Belt and Road Initiative, as nearly the entire rest of the world has done, provides the necessary basis for creating the new world order based on peace and development.

Macron has taken a major step to accomplish these three measures—although you certainly would not know it by reading the Western press.

On the first, Macron noted that China "has managed to lift 700 million people out of poverty in recent decades. This is true for France too, where we are confronted with mass unemployment, with the imperative

Xinhua/Zhang Duo

Chinese President Xi Jinping (L) holds a welcoming ceremony for visiting French President Emmanuel Macron before their talks in Beijing, capital of China, Jan. 9, 2018.

needed to give future prospects to a whole part of our population, but it is a challenge of the world that lives today in a crisis of globalized capitalism, which has, in recent decades, exploded social inequalities and the concentration of wealth."

On the strategic side, Macron said the West must overcome the "unilateral imperialism" conducted by France and other European powers in Africa and elsewhere, adding: "We must draw the lessons of the past. Every time we tried to impose the 'truth' or the 'law' against the people themselves, we were wrong, and sometimes we have produced an even worse situation, such as in Iraq, or Libya today. We need to work together to develop the respect of sovereignty of the people."

He spoke directly against the geopolitical paradigm dominating Western thought: "There should be neither a disguised supremacy, nor a conflict between competing supremacies. All our art, if I may use that word, will not be the art of war, but an art of cooperation, balanced in order to ensure on the geostrategic, political, and economic level, the harmony our world needs."

He referred to the West as a "tired, post-modern world, where the great epics were forbidden."

And most importantly, Macron identified the New Silk Road as the connection required between all peoples to achieve this new world order. "I think that the initiative of the New Silk Roads," he said, "can meet our interests, those of France and of Europe, if we give ourselves the means to really work together.... It is up to Europe and Asia, up to France and China, to define and propose together the rules of a game in which we will all win, or we will all lose. I have come thus to tell China my determination to have the Euro-Chinese partnership enter into the 21st Century with this new grammar we must all define together."

He praised China's work in Africa, where "China has invested heavily in recent years, in infrastructure, raw materials, with a financial force that European countries do not have." He called for French-Chinese cooperation in Africa, to "carry out projects that are really useful for the growth of the continent, financially sustainable—because the future is there, because we must not reproduce the mistakes of the past of creating political and financial dependence, under the pretext of development."

Most of the Western press, if they cover the visit at all, foolishly portray it as "anti-Trump," or a lecture to China to open its markets. This again demonstrates that Western leaders and their media spokespersons are unwilling, or unable, to part with their geopolitical glasses, their zero-sum, Darwinian mentality.

Helga Zepp-LaRouche, reflecting on Macron's extraordinary visit, noted that those nations which fail to join in the New Silk Road will be left behind in history. Yet the winds of historical change are blowing in the direction of this New Paradigm. President Trump has embraced China's crucial role in history and for the future; Japanese Prime Minister Shinzo Abe has pledged to co-finance projects with China along the New Silk Road; and now France is breaking from the resistance to the New Silk Road coming from the EU, and from Germany in particular.

EIR**Contents**

www.larouchepub.com Volume 45, Number 2, January 12, 2018

Cover This Week

Lyndon LaRouche demonstrates the principle of the Triple Curve.

I. The Choice Before America

Decision Time for U.S. Economy

by Harley Schlanger

Jan. 5—With all signs pointing toward increasing volatility in the trans-Atlantic financial markets, President Donald Trump must decide in the next weeks whether he will return to his campaign pledge to move against the destructive speculative policies of Wall Street financiers and their neo-liberal theorists, who are urging him instead to "stick with what is working." They are referring to the run-up of stock markets to record levels, and official dishonest statistics which claim to show a continuing decline of unemployment, which the President is touting as proof that his economic policies are working.

In reality, the record-setting stock market levels are not at all the result of improved profitability or productivity of corporations. Instead, they have been fueled by nearly interest-free credit, that banks and their blue-chip clients have been using for stock buybacks and speculative trading, rather than investing in the physical economy. As for unemployment, although the latest official unemployment figures claim the rate is 4.1%, the labor participation rate shows that only 62.7% of the potential workforce is currently employed. Among those encouraging the President to stay the course are the Goldman Sachs alumni in the administration, Treasury Secretary Mnuchin, who made huge profits cashing in on foreclosures resulting from the popping of the mortgage-backed securities bubble in 2008, and Gary Cohn, the director of the National Economic Council.

Many of the Wall Street neo-liberals and speculators benefitting most from the increased flow of funds into the stock market not only opposed Trump during his campaign, but have played a leading role in disrupting his presidency with the fraudulent narrative of Russia-gate to constrain him, to prevent him from carrying out his campaign pledges. You might say they are "betting

The New York Stock Exchange.

CGTN

White House/Ricky Harris

Treasury Secretary Steven Mnuchin.

White House/Evan Walker

Gary Cohn, Director of the National Economic Council.

the house" that they can keep him on this course, and away from the anti-Wall Street insurgency that carried him into the White House. What they fear most is not Trump's populist anti-Wall Street rhetoric, but that he might implement anti-Depression policies similar to those of Franklin D. Roosevelt, which have been revived by economist Lyndon LaRouche, in his Four New Laws.

During his presidential campaign, Trump was correctly critical of Hillary Clinton, who cited the same fake statistical trends of stock appreciation and declining official unemployment, to claim that there had been a "remarkable, robust economic recovery" under Barack Obama, and that she would continue those policies. Candidate Trump accused her of ignoring the plight of the "forgotten men and women," who lost jobs, homes, and savings in the 2008 crash, and have not benefitted from the speculative bubble created by the Bush and Obama bailouts after the crash, bailouts which gave trillions of dollars to bankrupt banks and the "shadow banking system," while denying credit for investment in job-creating manufacturing, construction, and business enterprises.

President Trump will have an opportunity for an economic "re-set" on Jan. 30, when he delivers the State of the Union address. Prior to that event, he will be holding meetings to finalize his long-awaited infrastructure plans. He is under enormous pressure from Wall Street speculators to limit infrastructure investment to public-private partnerships (PPPs), which their promoters argue can generate profits for them, while avoiding the problem of deficit spending. PPPs focus primarily on investing in low-cost projects with exist-

ing technology, such as privatizing roadways and constructing toll booths, which involve little cost, but hefty returns.

While Trump has disparaged PPPs, with an aide saying they are no "silver bullet," and do not reflect his desire for the most modern, high-tech infrastructure projects, he is being lobbied heavily by the Republican "deficit hawks" in Congress, led by Speaker of the House Paul Ryan and the "Freedom Caucus," to limit spending on infrastructure in order to reduce government outlays. Ryan and his coterie are also pressuring Trump to renege on his campaign pledge to protect Social Security and Medicare, as part of their broad austerity assault against so-called entitlements.

If he listens to these spokesmen for anti-government, "free market," austerity policies, which include further deregulation of banking and finance, it is inevitable that the stock and corporate debt bubbles, now ballooning to record levels, will pop, ushering in a deeper depression than that of 2008. As the sometimes insightful *New Yorker* magazine financial columnist John Cassidy wrote in October last year, if the President claims responsibility for the "Trump bull market," he could "end up owning the 'Trump Crash'...."

Trump vs. Wall Street on the Campaign Trail

In his campaign, Trump rarely missed an opportunity to attack Wall Street neo-liberals and their neo-conservative strategic allies for their policies of "endless bailouts and endless war," which cost "trillions of dollars and hundreds of thousands of lives." He ruthlessly attacked the free-trade economic agreements favored by Bush Republicans and Hillary Clinton Democrats, blaming them for a loss of manufacturing jobs—more than 6 million manufacturing jobs have been lost in the United States since 2001, in an extreme form of deindustrialization, through outsourcing.

One of his first acts as President was to pull the United States out of the Trans-Pacific Partnership (TPP), Obama's and Hillary Clinton's Asian "free trade" deal which excluded China, and would replace sovereign decisions on trade with rulings from globalist corporate-controlled courts. He repeatedly criticized

CSPAN

Presidential Candidate Donald Trump in Charlotte, North Carolina, Oct. 27, 2016.

those responsible for the speculation that caused the 2008 crash, calling JP Morgan Chase CEO Jamie Dimon "the worst banker in the U.S." He said that hedge fund managers are "getting away with murder" under the current tax code, and accused them of being "guys that shift paper around … and get lucky." Some of his sharpest comments against Hillary Clinton were related to the widespread support she enjoyed from Wall Street.

As for Obama, Trump correctly derided his claims of economic recovery, pointing out something repeatedly emphasized by LaRouche's weekly *Executive Intelligence Review* (*EIR*): that most of the jobs allegedly created by Obama were temporary, part-time and low wage; that real wages have been stagnant since the late 1980s; and that the labor participation rate showed that less than two-thirds of those eligible to work had jobs.

In July 2016, Trump shocked many when he insisted that the Republican Party platform include a call to restore Glass-Steagall banking regulation. His then campaign manager, Paul Manafort, said of this platform plank, "We also call for a reintroduction of Glass-Steagall, which created barriers between what big banks can do," adding that "the Obama-Clinton years have passed legislation that has been favorable to the big banks, which is why you see all the Wall Street money going to her. We are supporting the small banks and Main Street." Manafort has been the target of especially thuggish prosecution tactics by Russiagate special counsel Robert Mueller, including being hit with a bogus twelve-count indictment on Oct. 30, 2017.

Trump echoed this support for Glass-Steagall in a campaign speech delivered on Oct. 27, in Charlotte, North Carolina, when he said, "Equal justice also means the same rules for Wall Street. The Obama Administration never held Wall Street accountable." He continued: "I will also pursue financial reforms to make it easier for young African-Americans to get credit to pursue their dreams in business and create jobs in their communities. Dodd-Frank has been a disaster, making it harder for small businesses to get the credit they need. The policies of the Clintons brought us the financial recession—through lifting Glass-Steagall, pushing subprime lending, and blocking reforms to Fannie Mae and Freddie Mac. It's time for a 21st-century Glass-Steagall and, as part of that, a priority on helping African-American businesses get the credit they need."

> "We also call for a reintroduction of Glass-Steagall, which created barriers between what big banks can do … the Obama-Clinton years have passed legislation that has been favorable to the big banks, which is why you see all the Wall Street money going to her. We are supporting the small banks and Main Street."
>
> Trump Campaign manager Paul Manafort, July 2016

Fake Economics vs. Real Economy

After hitting a low of 6,500 in March 2009, the Dow Jones index of the New York Stock Exchange has appreciated wildly. While much of this occurred with Obama in office, the soaring of stock prices has continued under Trump, from 18,332 the day of his election, to crossing over 25,000 on Jan. 4, 2018. While this may be a cause for celebration for Wall Street traders and their blue-chip clients, is it good news for the real economy? According to banking historian and financial analyst Nomi Prins, corporate borrowing in the past was largely directed toward investment in "real growth," including new plant and equipment, research and development of new technologies, job hiring and training—in other words, investment which increased productivity, and allowed for an increase in the real wealth production capability of the firm. Instead, today, she writes that companies are using debt to go on a "spree of buying their own stock."

An estimate by *EIR* from March 2017 is that since 2013, 80% or more of corporate borrowing has gone to "financial engineering," i.e., buying one's own stock to drive up the price, or buying other companies' stock in mergers and acquisitions. This splurge of corporate debt has driven up stock values, even as the actual corporate profits are stagnant or falling. Total non-financial corporations' profits have not increased since 2011, while from 2013 to 2016, they dropped.

Yet during this time, total corporate debt has exploded, to over $14 trillion today, the bulk of which is owed to banks, money market mutual funds, and pension funds, for example. This is now substantially larger than the mortgage debt bubble, which was $11 trillion when it popped during 2007-08. In its Autumn 2017 report, the Bank for International Settlements (BIS) focused on the corporate debt bubble, warning that this level of debt is unsustainable. Its authors wrote about "zombie banks" and "zombie firms," defining them as "firms which could not survive without a flow of cheap financing." The BIS estimates that one of every ten corporations in the advanced countries and in emerging market countries is a "zombie," while the International Monetary Fund warns that even minimal increases in interest rates could doom 20% of corporations.

In her year-end forecast, Prins writes that "2018 will be a precarious year of more bubbles inflated by cheap money, followed by a leakage that will begin with bond or debt markets.... If there is another financial crisis in 2018 or later, it will be worse than the last one because the system remains fundamentally unreformed, banks remain too big to fail, and the Fed and other central banks continue to control the flow of funds to these banks (and through to the markets) by maintaining a cheap cost of funds."

Rein in Speculators, Extend Credit

In her recent weekly webcasts, the President of the German Schiller Institute, Helga Zepp-LaRouche, has

Andrew Jackson's British-steered populist campaign, leading to the destruction of Hamilton's Bank of the United States.

emphasized that a crash is not inevitable, if the policy solutions proposed by her husband in his "Four Laws" are applied, and the monetarist bubble policies of the financial oligarchy are rejected.

Mr. LaRouche's expertise is in physical economics, and he has spent a lifetime advancing the science of physical economy, drawing upon great scientific thinkers, such as Gottfried Leibniz, Benjamin Franklin, and Alexander Hamilton, who applied their genius to overcoming the false limits set by those who approached economy from the standpoint of "money," "trading" and "profit."

For these thinkers, it is human creativity which generates the advances in productivity, which uniquely allow for the rate of increase in the production of wealth, which can enable an ever-growing population to achieve an ever-improving standard of living. This "American System," which was elaborated in 1790-91 by Alexander Hamilton in four reports to the U.S. Congress, laid the basis for all future prosperity in the United States.

In these reports, Hamilton established a system which regulated the creation of currency and credit, acting through a National Bank, which directed credit to investments to improve the economic platform of the country, improving infrastructure, and promoting manufactures, to allow for maximum efficiency in the production and distribution of goods. Hamilton's policies, with the full support of President George Washington, enabled our young American republic to not only retire its Revolutionary War debts, but to launch a revolution in industrial and agricultural productivity, designed to promote, not individual consumption and accumulation of wealth, but the common good, or General Welfare, as defined in the Preamble to the Constitution.

This system was under attack from its beginnings, as the British Empire, reeling from the loss of its American colonies, attempted to destroy the Hamiltonian system. Hamilton himself was assassinated by a British operative, Aaron Burr, while elitist Anglophile bankers used the rage of "anti-bank, anti-government" populists to shut down Hamilton's Bank of the United States. Throughout American history, whenever the London-linked speculators succeeded in overturning Hamiltonian national credit policies—as in Andrew Jackson's action to shut down the second Bank of the United States, the overturning of Lincoln's Greenback credit policy, or the chipping away of FDR's New Deal—their victories led to the creation of new speculative bubbles, which eventually popped, ushering in depressions, destroying the lives of millions.

City of London/Wall Street swindlers mobilized throughout the 1980s and 1990s to remove FDR's Glass-Steagall bank separation act, finally succeeding in 1999. Their "success" over the years, in removing sections of Glass-Steagall, led to bubbles of various sorts, which popped in 1987, again in 1997, 1998 and 2000, and most recently in 2007-08. Each time, Lyndon LaRouche accurately forecast the collapse, while presenting an alternative. His alternative today, the "Four Laws," include restoring Glass-Steagall to shut down government/Central Bank protection of speculators, instead protecting savers and those who invest in the real physical economy; a Hamiltonian national credit policy, to fund real reconstruction of manufacturing and productive enterprises; full investment in necessary infrastructure, through a capital budget,

President Franklin Roosevelt signing the Glass-Steagall Act in June, 1933.

unrestricted by concerns for "budget deficits"; and funding science-driver projects, such as space exploration and the rapid development of nuclear fusion technology.

At times, as a candidate and as President, Donald Trump has spoken favorably about elements of this approach, even referring directly to the "American System" by name, and identifying key figures in the development of the American System, such as Hamilton, John Quincy Adams, Henry Clay, and Lincoln, as models for what he would like to do. His repeated reference to his desire to act to benefit the "forgotten men and women" echoes Franklin Roosevelt, who saved the nation from the Depression brought on by speculators and deregulators in the 1920s.

With the inventors of the Russiagate scandal increasingly weakened by exposure of their web of corruption, and before a new financial collapse of epic destruction occurs, it is now time for President Trump to revive the American System, in collaboration with China's Belt and Road Initiative. The whole purpose of Russiagate has been to prevent Trump from doing this. There is no time to waste—to pre-empt a new catastrophic global crash, and launch an American and global economic renaissance. LaRouche's Four Laws provide the ideal solution.

China Will End Poverty by 2020

by William Jones

Jan. 5—At the recently concluded 19th Congress of the Communist Party of China, the leadership committed itself to eliminate poverty by 2020, a centennial year when the Communist Party will be celebrating its 100th anniversary. Nothing like this has been accomplished by any country, ever. Yet there is little doubt but that China will succeed. China has already brought 700 million people out of poverty over the last two decades, and is maintaining a steady pace of bringing 10 million people a year out of poverty. And while China has no doubt accomplished this tremendous feat in the context of its own unique system, in which the Chinese Communist Party plays the dominant role, the real key is the absolute determination of its leadership, under Party General Secretary Xi Jinping, to make poverty alleviation the primary goal of government policy.

But can this also be accomplished in other countries, with different political systems and other cultural matrixes, one may ask? I think there is no doubt that with the same level of determination as that shown by the Chinese leadership, poverty *can* also be eliminated in other countries, even here in the United States, where poverty has grown rather than diminished over the last decades. The latest UN Report on Poverty in the U.S.A. indicates that there are 41 million Americans living in poverty (of a population of around 300 million) while in China, with a population of 1.3 billion people, there are only 30 million people still living in extreme poverty. By 2020, however, these people will be out of poverty—but for our 41 million, there is as yet still no light at the end of the tunnel. Our politicians would do well to study some of China's methods for dealing with this problem in order to give their own constituents the same hope that China is offering its citizens. All the particulars may be different, but if it can be done there, it can be done here.

Severe poverty in China today is now primarily limited to certain specific rural areas, often areas which

Xinhua/Liu Ailun

Hong Tianyun, Deputy Director of China's State Council Leading Group Office of Poverty Alleviation and Development of China (LGOP).

are very isolated and difficult to access. In 2013, President Xi Jinping had put forward the notion of "Targeted Poverty Alleviation," which pinpointed those areas and those groups that were severely impoverished, in order to develop a program to bring them out of poverty. A total of 320 departments were assigned to pair up with 592 destitute counties to help them out of poverty. In addition, 68 centrally administered state-owned enterprises assisted anti-poverty efforts in 108 impoverished counties in disadvantaged areas. And many of the developed provinces and cities in the more prosperous eastern part of the country supported the less developed areas in the West, providing funds, skilled professionals, innovative ideas, and business investment. Poverty reduction had become a national undertaking.

At a press briefing July 5, 2017, Hong Tianyun, the Deputy Director of the State Council Leading Group Office of Poverty Alleviation and Development, pointed to three geographical areas, three autonomous prefectures and three demographic groups that were still suffering from extensive poverty. The three areas were the Tibet Autonomous Region, the southern region of the Xinjiang Uyghur Autonomous Region, and the ethnic autonomous areas inhabited by Tibetans and other ethnic minority groups in Qinghai, Sichuan, Yunnan, and Gansu provinces. The three autonomous prefectures in extreme poverty were Linxia Hui Autonomous Prefecture in Gansu, the Liangshan Yi Autonomous Prefecture in Sichuan, and the Nujiang Lisu Autonomous Prefecture in Yunnan.

The three demographic groups affected by poverty were those who are impoverished because of illnesses—in particular, serious and chronic diseases—those who are impoverished as a result of natural disasters or because of market fluctuations, and the elderly poor, who because of their age or inability to work have to be supported by social insurance.

Xinhuanet file photo

A combine harvesting small grain in China. The government is providing financing for mechanization of agriculture.

Increasing Productivity in Agriculture

Much of the poverty reduction done in China has been an integral part of rural revitalization, a policy that was heavily emphasized at the 19th Party Congress. Much has been done through the years in terms of land reform in China. While all land is owned either by the central government or the local and provincial governments, farmers lease their plots from the government and these leases are generally long-term leases for around 30 years. Farmers migrating to the cities, seeking work to better support themselves and their families, most often leave behind their plots of land for their wives and children to work, but the small size of the plots means subsistence agriculture, at best. In the last few years, the Central Government has reformed the system considerably in order to allow migrant workers to sublease their land to other farmers who remain in the villages. These other farmers can then work the land, and often several landholdings can be combined, allowing for more effective utilization of these larger plots, as well as making it feasible to introduce machinery, farm equipment, and tractors.

Much effort is also being put into creating cooperatives in the villages. The land area of the farmers can be combined, and the government will often provide financing for machinery and fertilizer. Often young graduates from the colleges and universities will go out to the villages as entrepreneurs in order to help improve the local situation. Provided with financing, they can work to build a more effective agricultural operation. If they can persuade the villagers to transfer their land rights and participate as shareholders, they will be able to increase the output per hectare many times over, with the farm laborers now sharing in the profits as shareholders and also receiving a wage for their labor if they decide to also work the land. In some cases, the increased acreage can be concentrated on a particular crop which can then be marketed commercially to a much larger area than previously.

With the introduction of the Internet in the villages and e-commerce, as well as enhanced transportation with roads and railroads, the village farmers now enjoy a greater market for their product. In one typical instance, a young graduate arrived in the village of Dawangfu in Fengyang County in Anhui Province, and saw the miserable level of productivity in agriculture. He succeeded in getting the villagers to transfer their land rights and began growing greenhouse vegetables, flowers, and garden plants on an extended scale. His intensive regime and his increased use of new technology proved far more efficient than the old system, increasing output by as much as 500%.

Reclaiming the Land

There has also been a major drive toward land reclamation. In 2012 President Xi Jinping visited Fuping County, which is located in eastern Hebei Province, that borders Beijing. He told the villagers that the most arduous task facing China to complete the building of a moderately prosperous society is in rural areas, especially poverty-stricken regions. Reported in *Beijing Review,* Oct. 19, 2017, Xi noted that "a moderately prosperous society," the goal for 2020, cannot be achieved if the nation cannot create higher levels of prosperity in the rural districts. This visit undoubtedly created a new sense of vitality in the county. Baiyi Village is one village located in central Fuping. Fuping County has a population of around 2,400 people and only 76 hectares of arable land. A mountainous region, it also has well over 1,000 hectares of non-arable land. In 2015, more than half of the villagers lived below the national poverty line.

Agricultural experts came in to do a study of what measures could be taken to reclaim barren land. The villagers worked with them on their proposals and transferred their land-use rights on the barren plots, be-

Xinhua/Yang Shiyao

A farmer with tomatoes in a greenhouse in Dahuangzhuang village in China this year.

coming shareholders in the project. Much of the land was transformed into arable land through irrigation. By the end of 2016, 200 hectares of the mountainous region had been turned into arable land planted with apple trees, peach trees, cassia trees, peanuts, and sweet potatoes. The villagers earned a basic income of 1,000 yuan ($150) per household per month. Those who work for the venture by planting seeds or digging, can make an extra income of $450. When the project begins to pay off, the profits will be distributed between the investors and the villagers. By the end of 2020, when the land is expected to begin producing yields, each villager is expected to make a profit of more than $900.

The Key Role of Transportation

None of this could have been done without the tremendous investment in the transportation infrastructure in China, which now brings together what had been iso-

Xinhua/Zhan Yan

Modern housing being built Nanpingtouwu village in China this year.

Xinhua/Li Xiaoguo

Shoe production in Cuiyangzhuang village in China earlier this year.

pesticides. (See "Farming the World: China's Epic Race to Avoid a Food Crisis," Bloomberg, May 22, 2017.) And like the policy introduced in the United States by the Roosevelt Administration in the 1930s, the government also maintains a parity-price system for agricultural products in order to protect the income of the villagers from any sudden price fluctuations on the market.

The continued expansion of the social welfare system has also provided income for those villagers who are too old or physically unable to work. In his speech to the 19th Party Congress, President Xi promised to provide more support for the left-behind elderly in the villages. A nationwide pension system was established in 2009 which also included the rural aged, but developments locally are still very uneven, depending on the financial condition of the local governments. China has built 100,000 daycare and activity centers for the rural elderly and 110,000 community centers for the elderly in urban areas.

lated communities and allows the easy transport of their products to a wider market. At the end of December, President Xi issued a statement on the importance of building roads in the rural areas. A total of 1.275 million kilometers of rural roads have been built in the past five years, and about 99% of townships nationwide have access to buses, according to the Ministry of Transport. The construction of roads to the remote villages, the pumping of water to the households and to the fields for irrigation, as well as the introduction of electricity and modern farming equipment, and modern irrigation methods, has served to elevate the standard of life of the Chinese farmer.

As Bloomberg notes in an article on the subject: China's new breed of farmer isn't staring at the sky to predict rain. He's using a micro-irrigation system based on an array of soil sensors that feed data wirelessly to his smartphone. He's growing vegetables in climate-controlled shipping containers and using drones to apply computer-formulated doses of

The government is also encouraging the establishment of small businesses in the rural areas. The intro-

Xinhua/Lin Yiguang

Modern road in the rural area of Longtoushan Town in Ludian County, in China this year.

duction of the Internet into the rural townships has also had a tremendous impact, and e-commerce now allows small businesses to take orders from a larger target area than previously. Many university graduates, finding it difficult to get adequate employment in the cities, are attracted to the rural areas where they can set up small businesses and help the villages prosper.

This movement to the countryside is also promoted by the central government. It also helps to promote the development of new enclaves of small industry, often connecting to agricultural production, such as food processing, in the rural towns and counties. As structural reform is going at full speed in the cities, with the down-sizing of some of the heavy industries there, migrant workers can now return to their villages, where they can now find employment as laborers in the larger agricultural plots being formed, or in the burgeoning small industries developing in the rural villages and towns.

There is also a major construction program in many of the rural areas to provide decent and modern housing for the people in the villages. In some cases, where it is logistically impossible to maintain access to a village, villagers may be moved to a more accessible area where they can have access to the main commercial arteries of the region. President Xi noted that 3.4 million people have been moved in the course of the poverty alleviation campaign.

The rural revitalization is also an important collaboration between the central government, and the local and provincial governments, which often are more attuned to the needs and the requirements of the local areas and the local population. The specific conditions of the different localities sometimes forbid the application of a universal formula for creating economic growth in the region. The central and local authorities are in the process of cataloguing the impoverished households in a systematic way, in order to closely analyze the causes of their impoverishment and to find remedies for it. A meeting of the Leading Group for Deepening Overall Reform of the 19th CPC Central Committee on Nov. 20, which President Xi Jinping chairs, adopted guidelines on the selection and management of officials working in poverty-stricken areas, along with a three-year action plan on the rural environment, focusing on garbage and waste disposal while preserving the landscape. The group also called for expansion of a pilot project to reform rural residential land, which would protect public ownership of land, farmers' interests, and arable land.

Expanding the medical services in the rural areas is also an important element in eliminating extreme poverty. Speaking at a press conference on the sidelines of the 19th Party Congress, Li Bing, the chairman of the National Health and Family Planning Commission, said that 80% of the Chinese population were not more than 15 minutes from a medical clinic. But more remains to be done to improve the situation for the remaining 20%, primarily in the rural areas. The Leading Group in its meeting on Nov. 20, also called for improving the recruitment of general medical practitioners, especially in impoverished areas.

And while there is now universal education in China, the discrepancies between the quality of education in the cities and the countryside leave much to be desired. Here again, the expansion of university education over the last two decades has created a situation where many graduates have a difficult time finding employment in the larger cities. They are encouraged to move to the second- and third-tier cities and to the countryside, where they have a broad field for utilizing their education as teachers. And in both medicine and education, the expansion of the Internet has allowed for a much broader reach by the more qualified doctors and more capable teachers, to extend their reach to the rural areas.

This Chinese effort has become a clarion call to the countries of the developing sector. If China with its 1.3 billion people can eradicate poverty, it can also be done globally. And China's export of this model in the Belt and Road Initiative has created the basis for the world as a whole to move in that direction. What was once thought to be a laudable but unrealizable goal, is now seen as a realistic perspective for mankind. People in the West, and particularly here in the United States, simply have to begin to look at China and its development in an objective manner, rather than viewing China in the traditional zero-sum framework of geopolitics, where one man's loss is another man's gain. President Xi has introduced the building of "a community of common destiny for mankind" as a "win-win" solution to the problems of the world. It's time for the United States to become a winner as well, and contribute to the building of such a community.

Russia, China, U.S.A. New Silk Road Collaboration

by Michael Billington

The following is an edited transcript of remarks by EIR *Asia Editor Mike Billington to a national organizers' conference call of the LaRouche PAC on Dec. 28. His projection that major progress towards Korea negotiations was close at hand, despite belligerent statements from President Trump and Kim Jung-un, has been borne out by the opening of talks on Jan. 3 between North and South Korea, and Trump's announcement Jan. 4 that scheduled military exercises with South Korea would be postponed until after the Winter Olympics, as had been requested by Seoul.*

I'll say a word about Korea, because everybody is talking about Korea—all the headlines are that the world is on the brink of war in Korea, that Trump is making belligerent threats, and that Kim Jung-un is making belligerent threats. The reality, I think, is quite different. The reality is that Trump, in his typical way, believes that when you negotiate you have to be a tough guy. I don't particularly approve of that, but that's the way he is. And the idea that he and Secretary of State Rex Tillerson are at odds with each other is nonsense. It's clear that Trump knows very well what Tillerson is doing when Tillerson says the United States is willing to negotiate with North Korea without pre-conditions, and that when he pledges to the North Koreans that we will not invade, we will not have regime change, he means it.

The question, really, is will the North Koreans believe it? They have seen what happened to Iraq, and they saw what happened to Libya, after Libya gave up its nuclear weapons program and was promptly bombed back to the stone age: Leaders of both countries were killed. So the question in my mind is, if the North Koreans are going to believe it, it's only going to be because they also believe that the

United States is, in fact, working with Russia and China—not just in negotiating or imposing sanctions on North Korea, but working with them sincerely, everywhere in the world. If they see that this New Paradigm is in place, then they have a basis for believing that they can talk, and that they can talk in terms of eventually changing their whole nuclear posture—but on the basis of being part of the New Silk Road, of being part of the development of the Russian Far East, and of becoming part of a great development process sweeping across the world.

So all of this is imminently possible, if we defeat the Mueller coup, if Trump is in fact allowed to proceed with his intention of working with Russia and China.

The worst hotspots globally are in Southwest Asia and Korea. These situations were created for a reason. In Southwest Asia, the British purposely created Israel

U.S. Secretary of State Rex Tillerson speaking at the State Dept. Dec. 21, 2017.

North Korea Head of State Kim Jung-un.

such that there would be a permanent, constant crisis between the Arabs and the Jews. They wanted that—they wanted that as a cockpit for war, where everyone would have to line up—either you are with the Israelis, or you are with the Palestinians. This is the East versus the West, a perfect cockpit for keeping the imperial global division of East versus West alive.

Korea is the same thing. The Korean crisis *was solved,* in 1994, under the Bill Clinton Administration. Clinton had, along with Bill Perry who was his Defense Secretary and a few other decent people, basically solved the problem. Under what was called the Agreed Framework—the North Koreans shut down their nuclear weapons program, and shut down their nuclear plant that produced plutonium, and agreed to let the West build a safer nuclear plant and to send in some oil, and agreed to have IAEA monitors all over the country to make sure they didn't build any weapons. It was all solved. And it was moving ahead—slowly, but it was moving ahead—until Bush and Cheney got elected and scrapped the whole thing. They said, we don't like North Korea and we believe they are cheating, so we're going to cancel this program—even though their own Secretary of State, Colin Powell, said it was working well and it should be maintained.

What did this reversal do? It meant the North Koreans went back to their nuclear weapons program. By being hostile, the policy was, "Go ahead and build a bomb." Then when Obama came in, he had a policy called "strategic patience," which was: we're not going to talk to you until you do what we say. So, of course, what's the real policy behind this? "Go ahead and build

your bomb!" Why?

Because the British empire needed a cockpit for war. They needed an excuse for Obama's pivot to Asia, the isolation of China, and the military ring around China and Russia, all under the guise of, "Oh, we're defending ourselves against North Korea." Well, you don't need much to defend against North Korea. This military deployment is not aimed at North Korea—it's aimed at China and Russia.

The British imperial policy of keeping the world divided depends upon such hot spots.

That said, what's going on now? If you have Russia and the United States and China openly, publicly collaborating on the New Silk Road, and on strategic wars against terrorism in Syria and elsewhere, if this is open and public, the way that Lyndon and Helga LaRouche have fought for this for the last fifty years, then there is no reason for the existence of these hot spots. They no longer have a purpose in the world. In other words, the British empire's game is finished.

And the Korean hotspot will be resolved, not through some political wheeling and dealing with North Korea alone, but through the New Silk Road global paradigm shift, which gives everyone the confidence that we can trust each other, that we are working together as human beings, and therefore that these seemingly intractable and dangerous situations can be resolved.

President Clinton meeting high level north Korean military officer, Jo Myong-rok, 2000.

Now We Can Move to A New Era of Civilization

This is an edited transcript of Helga Zepp-LaRouche's Schiller Institute Webcast of Jan. 4, 2018.

Harley Schlanger: Hello, I'm Harley Schlanger from the Schiller Institute. Welcome to this week's Schiller Institute international webcast, featuring our President and founder Helga Zepp-LaRouche.

Helga, in your New Year's greeting, you stated that there is reason for optimism this year because solutions do exist. It is only necessary to make sure these solutions are implemented. As we will discuss today, there have been very significant developments on a broad range of fronts, including the new exposures that promise the possibility of ending the Mueller investigation. There's the new opening between North and South Korea, as a channel of communications was opened, that is certainly promising; and continuing developments with the Belt and Road Initiative from China.

Let's begin with the situation in the United States. In the so-called Russiagate, there's a new book that came out called *Fire and Fury: Inside the Trump White House,* by Michael Wolff, which has the typical stink of a British smear-job. But it's opened the door to an interesting backlash. What do you make of this book and the recent Russiagate developments?

Helga Zepp-LaRouche: I think this book is full of inaccuracies and lies, but it actually had one very positive effect, because it quotes former counselor to President Trump, Steve Bannon, attacking Trump. Now, Bannon had come out in the recent period very strongly anti-China and anti-Russia. Trump responded with a White House message completely distancing himself from Bannon, and that has caused a complete storm.

But these are really side shows. Some-

thing much, much more important is going on, and to begin with, I would like all our viewers and listeners to absolutely make sure that you switch on your livestream connection to larouchepac.com at 7 p.m. tomorrow, because there will be a truly important meeting including the whistleblowers from the Veteran Intelligence Professionals for Sanity (VIPS), William Binney and Ray McGovern, and also Barbara Boyd, who is famous for having written the *EIR* dossier on Robert Mueller. They will reveal why all of these lies are very dangerous and could potentially lead to war with Russia. This meeting of three of probably the best experts on the subject you can imagine, is coming in the context of the whole Russiagate hoax falling apart.

While the mainstream media are still trying to change the subject by focussing on this Wolff book and on the Bannon story, the real important story instead is what happened yesterday. Remember that on Dec. 28, Congressman Devin Nunes, the chairman of the House Intelligence Committee, issued an ultimatum to the FBI and the Department of Justice to release all documents

WWW.NEWS.CN

Steve Bannon, former counselor to President Trump.

C-SPAN

Deputy Attorney General Rosenstein and FBI Director Wray were forced into an agreement with House Speaker Paul Ryan.

C-SPAN

next couple of days all the documents pertaining to this story that he had requested, would be released.

Now, I'll only believe it when I actually see that these documents are really there, but Nunes is now very confident that all the documents will be released. This is a breaking story, because I'm absolutely certain that once these documents are in the hands of the House Intelligence Committee, or the Senate Judiciary Committee, where Senator Grassley is involved in a similar investigation, then this can boomerang! The real story here is not that Russia was colluding with the Trump campaign. The real scandal is that if it turns out that the Obama Administration colluded with British intelligence and the Hillary Clinton campaign and the DNC, in order to conspire against an opposing candidate—and after he won the election, against an elected President, that is a scandal which could totally dwarf the Watergate scandal. This is now the breaking story.

So don't be confused by what the mainstream media are trying to sell you as the key story, because the true story is what Rep. Nunes and Sen. Grassley are now pursuing.

relating to the activities involving the DOJ and the FBI with respect to the dossier of Christopher Steele, the so-called "former" MI6 agent, whose dossier is the ground upon which this Russiagate story was built.

Now, this story is falling apart.

There was another absolutely desperate effort by Glenn Simpson and Peter Fritsch, the head and founders of the Fusion GPS firm—the firm that hired Christopher Steele in the first place—with a Jan. 2 op-ed in the *New York Times* in which they try to defuse the whole story, by saying what a heroic job they did in protecting the United States from a terrible Russian onslaught in the 2016 presidential campaign. But none of this is working, because the truth is coming out. Yesterday FBI Director Christopher Wray and Deputy Attorney General Rod Rosenstein went to see House Speaker Paul Ryan to discuss the Nunes request with him. Shortly afterwards, Nunes released a statement stating that he had an agreement in hand ensuring that in the

Schlanger: You made the point that there was a desperate attempt to cover this up by the two founders of Fusion GPS. In their statement, they essentially said that the work that they did "proved" that there was Russian intervention, and they spoke in the op-ed as if there was actual proof that had been presented. But, as Bill Binney, Ray McGovern, and Barbara Boyd will present tomorrow evening, no proof has been presented, and this why the whole story is falling apart.

Also, Helga, I think it's important that former Trump campaign manager Paul Manafort, who was one of the people who was targetted by Mueller, has filed a civil action to have his case dropped, because he claims it's outside of the range of the Special Counsel's mandate.

In the midst of all this, the State of the Union address is coming up at the end of the month and we have new warnings of a financial crisis. How does this play out? If Trump could be freed from this operation, what could potentially happen with the economy in the coming weeks?

Zepp-LaRouche: The warnings of Roger Stone that the cabal which is trying to get rid of Trump will not give up, have to be taken very seriously. Just now, I think 56 congressmen are cosponsoring a bill to see if they can pursue the 25th Amendment against Trump, and they're trotting out all kinds of psychiatrists who try to interpret Trump's tweets and find reasons that he's not fit to be President. I mean, it looks quite different: If Trump is freed from the Russiagate scandal, which is about to happen; if Trump is freed from the populist scenario which Bannon was associated with—and in his message, Trump said he was elected by the forgotten men and women, and he answers to them, not Bannon.

So, if these two chokepoints are removed from Trump, then the field is totally open. And there are now various conservative news blogs and others who are pointing out that the idea that you create jobs with the tax reform doesn't work—you *need* Glass-Steagall! So if even some from the conservative Republican circles are demanding Glass-Steagall, this is very important. And our colleagues in the United States, colleagues from LaRouche PAC, are involved in a major campaign to distribute the Four Laws of Lyndon LaRouche. The first law is to re-establish Glass-Steagall. Then go to a Hamiltonian credit system. The United States should join the New Silk Road. This is the campaign which allows us to say that there are solutions—because it would be very easy, once you have a clear perspective, to go for a massive infrastructure program. The big battle right now, as far as I can see, is in the Republican Party, where the neocons and the people close to Wall Street want to prevent that from happening, and instead pursue cutting entitlements and the like.

So the crucial battle is really in the remaining three weeks before the State of the Union address. Everyone who is concerned, should see, on the other side, the tremendous momentum of the New Silk Road. Even people who have been distant and have been warning against the New Silk Road, are now saying, "forget all the reservations; this is the big game in town, it's the only show in town; it's the largest infrastructure program in the history of the planet." It should be obvious that any country which does not work with the New Silk Road will be sidelined.

There are tremendous strategic realignments going on right now, and as a former German Ambassador to China just wrote in a long article in a German economic newspaper, the people who say that the relationship of Europe to the United States and China is a zero-sum game are completely wrong, because you can simultaneously have a very good relationship with the United States, and with China. Those who have reservations are obviously only projecting their own hegemonic intentions from the previous century onto China. This former Ambassador, Michael Schaefer, goes on to say that he knows Chinese President Xi Jinping personally from previous years, and that he is a totally calm person with long vision, with an idea of a harmonious development—and people should just join it.

And there are more and more voices of even bankers, who now say, "No, this is the new game in town." So if the United States can be brought to join this New Silk Road, and Chinese investments in infrastructure in the United States can take place—I mean, China is a champion at this! They already now have 25,000 km of high-speed rail; they're planning to have 38,000 km by the

Photo courtesy of Fluor Corp.

A massive infrastructure program needs Glass-Steagall: U.S. Army Corps of Engineers works on repairing power lines near San Juan, Puerto Rico as part of rebuilding the island's electrical system months after the destruction of Hurricane Maria.

year 2030. They will soon connect every major city in China through a high-speed rail system. Why can't that be done in the United States? The conditions in the United States demand a complete renewal of infrastructure. The *Pittsburgh Post-Gazette* had a very good article recently, noting that Atlanta's airport, which is the world's largest hub for air traffic, closed down for eleven hours because of an electricity blackout due to aging infrastructure, and that that is the condition of most of the electrical grid in the United States, because the infrastructure in the United States is aging, it's 50, 60, or 100 years old—bridges, roads, all of this needs to be repaired.

But this cannot be repaired, it cannot be financed, if you stay within the rules of Wall Street. Therefore, the big battle is how to get President Trump to stick to his election promises, reinstating Glass-Steagall and the American System of economy of Lincoln, Carey, and Alexander Hamilton. That is what we have to get on the agenda, and then all the problems can be solved.

Xinhua/Wang Lei

Traders at the New York Stock Exchange.

How to Prevent the Coming Crash

Schlanger: On that note, Helga, there's also the question of Lyndon LaRouche's Four Laws as the basis for this, versus this fake economics from Wall Street. The President is, I think, mistakenly talking about the stock market as an indicator of the economy. You were talking earlier about the warnings coming out internationally, with debt bubbles and financial crises. It would seem that this would be the incentive, given this danger of a crash, to go back to these campaign promises, wouldn't it?

Zepp-LaRouche: Yes. As the year is just starting, a lot of analysts from around the world, including from China, are warning of new "black swans" in the financial system. Nomi Prins and many other analysts, and bankers from many countries are warning that there is a 100% certainty that this system will crash. It's very difficult to say exactly when it could crash, whether at the beginning of this year, or a little bit later, but the parameters are all much, much worse than 2008—the corporate debt bubble is much bigger, the indebtedness of the states, student loans, car loans, the real estate situation, all the parameters. Naturally, the derivatives exposure is about one-third to one-half larger than in 2008. The difference now, is that all the so-called "instruments" of the central banks have been used up, and the only thing left is money-pumping. Despite the fact that inflation is not yet so visible, except in the stock market, hyperinflation is a definite possibility. And the stock market—it's a bubble. People should not think that that is an indicator of the health of the economy. If you look at the jobs, at how many people are now omitted from labor statistics, at the suicide rates and the drug epidemic—all of these are factors affecting the real economy, and that has not yet been addressed.

So the pressing need is to really go for a real, Roosevelt-style infrastructure program with the Four Laws of LaRouche—which involves a lot of physical science. It involves a crash program for fusion power and for space technology. We need a real discussion about these matters very urgently, in the next two to three weeks.

Schlanger: And this, of course, is something that our listeners can do something about, by working to ensure that these issues are discussed, that we're not trapped in the fake economic reporting of the mainstream media.

The other significant development on the strategic side of things, was the opening of communications between North Korea and South Korea. This is something that promises the possibility of moving out of this threat of nuclear confrontation. What do you know about this, Helga?

Zepp-LaRouche: I think it is a promising development, because the dialogue has been started. It's not entirely clear on what level it will be actually be conducted, but rumors are also that South Korea and the United States have suspended military training and drills during the time of the upcoming Winter Olympics in South Korea, and it is a promising thing. Because if the two Koreas talk to each other, the ice is broken. And I think D.P.R.K. Chairman Kim Jong-un is doing it from a position of strength, because he says that North Korea is now a full-fledged nuclear power, so nobody can attack North Korea without paying a terrible price for it. And this is because he looked at Saddam Hussein, at Qaddafi, and at what was attempted against Bashar Assad, and that is why he pursued nuclear weapons.

So I think if we get away from that kind of immediate danger of confrontation, and South Korea resumes the Sunshine Policy of Kim Dae-jung, in the context of the New Silk Road, along with Putin's promise to help in the development of North Korea if they are willing to denuclearize, and China offering Silk Road cooperation—I think we are entering a period where that problem can be brought under control, and I think this is very promising.

And I think the views of U.S. Ambassador to the UN Nikki Haley, who says she doesn't care about the two Koreas talking, are just completely wrong! It's a completely arrogant view, because after all, it's the Korean Peninsula which is at stake and the people living there. So, I think it's a very good and promising development.

Schlanger: And of course, Nikki Haley is tied to people like John Bolton and the same neo-cons who were responsible for the Iraq War and the chaos in the Middle East.

At the same time, we're seeing a potentially disturbing trend, coming not so much from Iran, but from commentary about Iran, that there may be a regime change under way. What do you know about this situation in Iran, right now?

Zepp-LaRouche: Well—It's a little bit too early to make a definite judgment. What seems to be clear is that the unrest erupted because some mullahs were caught in speculation, where people lost some investments in hedge funds—and then quickly that protest turned from

UN photo/Evan Schneider

Nikki Haley, U.S. Ambassador to the UN.

people being furious about having lost their savings into demanding a total change of the mullahs. And now there is a claim that the MEK was involved in it, pushed by Saudi Arabia.

Now, the MEK (Mujahideen-e-Khalq) was on the U.S. terrorist list until 2012, when Hillary Clinton took them off. But it was regarded as a terrorist organization, and it's very clear that whether they were the originators, or if they just jumped on the bandwagon, in any case, now the British, Saudi Arabia, and unfortunately a large part of the Trump administration, including Trump himself, have encouraged this unrest.

I think this is very dangerous, because if there is civil war in Iran, or even destabilization, a Syria-like situation in Iran, that would be a disaster wanted by no one. On the other side, if the New Silk Road is extended from China to Iran, which is already under way, then it can be extended to Iraq, to Syria, to Egypt, to Turkey, to Europe, to Africa. That's really the question—and Iranian President Rouhani received President Xi Jinping almost three years ago, and they agreed that the New Silk Road/Belt and Road Initiative should be extended to Iran and beyond. I think that this is a very dangerous development, because if you have a destabilization, the whole Iran deal could go out the window, and we'll be back to the question of building nuclear weapons. Right now, this is really the most dangerous spot in my view.

So people should really not fan the flames, because

Chinese President Xi Jinping (R) with Iranian President Hassan Rouhani in Iran in 2016.

the benefit of all—but that is *exactly* the debate which we have to have. And since the New Silk Road is such a strong dynamic, I think it can be realized: It just needs to be discussed, we have to have a political discourse about these questions, and show a willingness to move to new era of civilization.

Schlanger: One of the areas which we see as a bright spot for this "win-win" policy is Africa, where some of these projects are now coming online. You told me earlier that there's now an agreement for Japan to work with China in Africa. What's your perspective on what we can expect in the next period with this cooperation in Africa?

this is just a continuation of the previous British/Saudi policies. When it was clear that ISIS was defeated in Syria and in Iraq, there were offers to extend the Silk Road into Afghanistan via Iran. It's really the question of whether there can be peaceful development, so that these countries can be reconstructed. Are geopolitical forces at work trying to prevent exactly that?

And I think that people should really help to rebuild the Middle East, because these people have suffered so much from wars which were based on lies. Just think how many millions of people have lost their lives, and how much misery has been created. Look at what's happening in Yemen right now: the worst genocide, with seven million people in acute danger of losing their lives! The world community *must* become adult and stop these games—and that is why I said in my New Year's greetings, that of all the many things which have to be straightened out, geopolitics must stop! Geopolitics in the age of thermonuclear weapons cannot be a way to conduct policy. Xi Jinping has established a new paradigm, with the idea of a new, shared community for the shared future of mankind, a community of common destiny. By doing that, he has established a higher level of relations among countries which is not based on geopolitics.

I think people have to think that through, because people in the West are so accustomed to think that policy is a zero-sum game: If one wins, the other loses—that we cannot have a world where everybody cooperates to

Zepp-LaRouche: I think this is one of the most interesting things, because Japan has not only expressed a total willingness to cooperate with the Belt and Road Initiative, with the Asian Infrastructure Investment Bank (AIIB) in a bilateral relation between China and Japan—but Japan has also offered, for the first time, to cooperate with China in the development of four major projects in Africa. Now, this is exactly what the New Silk Road Spirit can bring about: That you not only have bilateral relations of "win-win" cooperation, but that countries which have major industrial capacities like China and Japan, can unite for the benefit of third countries, or in this case even of an entire continent, and help to overcome underdevelopment.

And that is what the United States should join in, and so should the Europeans. Right now there are many countries in Europe which are coming on board, but some others are not. The visit of French President Emmanuel Macron to China on Jan. 8 will be very interesting in this context. French Economics Minister Bruno Le Maire just gave an interview in which he said Macron's intention is to build an economic backbone from Paris to Moscow to Beijing. If that is the outcome of Macron's visit, then you will have Eastern Europe, Central Europe, the Balkan countries, Southern Europe, and France all moving in this direction, and that would make the position of the European Union and of the non-existent government in Berlin very isolated. As I have been saying the whole time, anyone who doesn't get on board with this new para-

French President Emmanuel Macron's state visit to China holds great promise for Europe's partnership in the New Silk Road. Here, President Macron and the First Lady are hosted at China's cultural treasure, the Terracotta Warriors and Horses of Emperor Qin Shihuang in Xi'an.

digm, will be sidelined by history, at a great peril for their people.

The solutions are so close. Therefore there is reason to be tremendously optimistic that this year, 2018, can witness a very, very positive change in the history of mankind, where we leave these geopolitical confrontations behind us, and establish a concert of nations working for the common good.

I know many people may think this is all completely idealistic and unrealistic—but look at what China *is doing*: China is going global. There is a new spirit, which was expressed by Xi Jinping and others at the Belt and Road Forum last May. It was reiterated at the 19th National Congress of the Chinese Communist Party in October. It was expressed by Xi Jinping, and Chinese Foreign Minister Wang Yi and others in their New Year's speeches; and China is now moving with incredible speed to go global. It's happening on all levels, and there's no reason to feel threatened by it, because if countries such as Germany or the United States were to return to their best traditions, like the United States going back to the Kennedy Apollo idea, or going back to the New Deal of Roosevelt, there is nothing which the United States and China cannot do together; or Germany and China, or other countries working together.

People have to change their thinking! It's not a zero-sum game. It's the idea of asking—can we define goals for humanity, can we do what was discussed in the *Federalist Papers* when America was young? Can we find the form of self-rule which ensures long-term survivability of our society? I think we can. I think the human species is capable of reason. I think we are even capable of love—and people think love has nothing to do with politics, but that's not true! The outcome of the Thirty Years' War was a terrible destruction in Europe, but out of that came the Peace of Westphalia. And if you look at the principles of the Peace of Westphalia, the two most important features were, first, for the sake of peace, forget every evil which was done by one side or the other, and concentrate on joint development. The second principle was, for the sake of peace, foreign policy from now on has to be based on "the interest of the other," and love.

And I think that that is what China is doing: It's consistent with the idea of the harmonious development of all nations—and that was the policy of John Quincy Adams, so it's not alien to American history. It was also associated with humanism in Europe, with the ideas of Leibniz, of Cusa, and of many other great people who thought in terms of development as the goal of history.

So we are at a crucial change of era, when we have to leave the era of geopolitics behind us and move to a completely new phase in the history of civilization.

Schlanger: Helga, I think you just summarized very beautifully why we can be optimistic as we approach this year. *But!* optimism alone won't do it: We have to be active. And I call on all of our listeners and supporters to make sure that this is the year you become members of the Schiller Institute and become active with us, so that we can ensure that these policy solutions will be implemented.

So Helga, until next week, thank you very much, and we'll see you then.

Zepp-LaRouche: OK, bye.

The Alexandrov Ensemble Remembered: One Year Later

by Diane Sare

Jan. 8—"On December 25, 2016, the Tu-154 plane of the Russian Ministry of Defense crashed in the Black Sea. There were 92 people on board, among them 64 artists of the Song and Dance Ensemble of the Defense Ministry named after Alexandrov. No one survived. The artists were flying to the New Year's concert to be held in the Syrian city of Aleppo.

"The Alexandrov Ensemble had almost 90 years of history and had become one of the brightest symbols of the USSR, and after that of Russia.

"Alexander Alexandrov, a composer and conductor, was also the author of the music for the Russian National Anthem. Although the words of the Russian anthem have changed three times in history, the music is still that written by Alexandrov."

Color Guard at the Tear Drop Memorial in Bayonne, N.J.

So began the short speech of Olga Zatsepina, President of the Russian American Cultural Heritage Center, at a concert in Manhattan on January 6 in memory of the Ensemble, and of all those who died in the crash that day.

The concert was the second of two events organized by the Schiller Institute NYC Chorus and, in the case of the concert, co-sponsored by the Foundation for the Re-vival of Classical Culture. The occasion was the first anniversary of the terrible crash which occurred in the middle of the holidays, and came quickly on the heels of the assassination of Russia's Ambassador to Turkey, who had been gunned down as he was giving a lecture in an art museum there.

This year, with the recent liberation of Syria from the Islamic State, the sacrifice made by those who perished in the crash has been answered by the "long arc of justice," with the potential to free that nation, and hopefully mankind, from the scourge of barbarism and war.

Earlier on that bitterly cold morning of January 6, a wreath-laying ceremony was held at the Tear Drop Memorial in Bayonne, N.J. This towering monument was a gift from the people of Russia to the American people, in memory of those who perished in the attacks of September 11, 2001.

In the memorial ceremony, directed by Captain Donald Haiber of the Bayonne Fire Department, a Color Guard from the New York Police Department and the Bayonne Fire Department Honor Guard presented the flags of the United States and Russia, as the Schiller Institute Chorus sang the Russian and American national anthems. Ray McGovern of the Veteran Intelligence Professionals for Sanity (VIPS) joined the chorus for the anthems, and World War II Veteran Al Korby was seated next to the podium. Deputy Permanent Representatives to the UN of both Russia and Syria were present and spoke from the podium.

In the sub-freezing temperature and blistering wind, the remarks were brief but profound. A transcript follows. Father John Fencik gave the invocation and requested that the chorus learn a Russian liturgical piece for the ceremony next year. Father Fencik, we later learned, is the nephew of a man who translated at the famous meeting of Americans and Soviets on the River Elbe in 1945.

Father John Fencik: Oh God of spirits and all flesh, who has conquered Satan and vanquished death, and granted life to your world, Lord give rest to the souls of your faithfully departed servants, the members of the Alexandrov Choir, who lost their lives on Christmas [one year ago]. Give them rest in a peaceful, serene place, from which all pain and sorrow and sighing are absent. As the good and gracious God Who loves mankind, forgive all transgressions committed by them in word or in thought, voluntarily as a human frailty. There is no man living who does not sin. You

LPAC TV

Captain Don Haiber, Bayonne Fire Department.

LPAC TV

Father John Fencik

LPAC TV

Petr Iliichev, First Deputy Permanent Representative of the Russian Federation to the United Nations.

alone are without sin. Your truth is truth for eternity, your word alone reality. For You are the Resurrection, the Life and the Repose for your departed servants, Oh Christ, our God. We rend You glory together, Eternal Father, holy, gracious and life-creating Spirit, always now and ever, and forever. Amen.

In blessed repose grant eternal rest, Oh Lord, to the souls of Your departed servants. Make eternal their memories, *Vechnaya pamyat! Vechnaya pamyat! Vechnaya pamyat!* [Eternal memory!]

Captain Donald Haiber: Please welcome Mr. Petr Iliichev, the First Deputy Permanent Representative of the Russian Federation to the UN.

First Deputy Representative Petr Iliichev: Friends, we gather today one year after the tragic events of 25th December 2016, when we lost the Alexandrov Ensemble, journalists, and humanitarian worker and philanthropist Elizaveta Glinka. We are still mourning the losses, which were terrible and tremendous, and we are grateful to the American who showed solidarity during those trying times. We are thankful to the Schiller Institute, the New York Police Department, and the Fire Department of Bayonne for organizing this event.

Time passes by, but the loss is still felt. But the best way to pay tribute to those courageous men and women who perished that night, is to remember them, and to continue their course.

In Russia, the Alexandrov Ensemble was reconstituted just two months after the tragedy. Now, new performers, new singers, new dancers were found. And they were found not only because of their merits, because of their voices, because of their craftmanship, but because of their moral qualities, because of their solidarity.

So, by summer, they performed in more than a dozen countries.

The charity foundation that was founded by Elizaveta Glinka is continuing its noble cause, helping people in need, sometimes under very difficult situations. It was decided that a public award named after Elizaveta Glinka will be established, and the first award will be made on the 20th of February, her birthday.

So, let's remember those people who are trying to show solidarity, to show sympathy with people all over the world, especially the people in Syria. And this year, Syria saw some positive changes. The so-called "Islamic State" was defeated, the Syrian parties have started talking to each other—talks in Astana, talks in Geneva continue. Now they are going to have a Congress of National Dialogue in Sochi, trying to bring an end to the civil war in Syria.

And again, the best tribute to those people who perished will be to remember them, may their souls rest in peace. Thank you!

Captain Haiber: Thank you. Now, I'd like to ask Deputy Permanent Representative Mounzer Mounzer, from the Syrian Mission to the UN, to speak.

Deputy Representative Mounzer Mounzer: Let me say that the disaster of losing the Alexandrov Ensemble, was not only a big national loss to the Russian

Mounzer Mounzer, Deputy Permanent Representative of Syria to the United Nations.

people and to the Russian government. It was, and it is, a big national loss to the Syrian people and to the Syrian government. We all know this ensemble was established about one century ago. All this time, the Alexandrov Ensemble was a partner in all the achievements of the Russia people along its struggle during this time.

We feel regret of course, and we are partners with the Russian people, because this ensemble gave their lives while they were on their way to celebrate with the Syrian people the victory against terrorism.

I will conclude to say, the Syrian people will never forget the Alexandrov Ensemble. We will never forget their sacrifice. They will remain forever living in our souls and in our consciousness, and may their souls rest in peace.

Thank you.

Captain Haiber: On behalf of the Bayonne Fire Department and the City of Bayonne, we want to thank everyone and welcome everyone participating today in this ceremony. A year ago today we gave our condolences to the families of the Alexandrov Ensemble and to the people of Russia. Everyone here proves, I believe, that this small remembrance shows our humanity towards one another, and God knows we could use more of that.

Once again, it is fitting we are here at the 9/11 Tear Drop Memorial, since the creator of this monument was the Russian sculptor Zurab Tsereteli. In the darkness after 9/11, this monument helps to bring peace and hope to many people who visit it. We now wish to pay that

Diane Sare

EIRNS/Joe Friendly

forward. This small token our sympathy, hopefully, will bring back a touch of hope and light to the Russian people.

On a personal level, I am honored to be here again, as I worked at Ground Zero, and this monument has personal meaning to me. May the peace and hope that I feel when I am here, be conveyed back to the people of Russia, and the families that have suffered this terrible loss. Music has meaning, and this quote from Billy Joel conveyed that better than anything I can say:

"I think music in itself is healing, it's an explosive expression of humanity. It's something we are all touched by. No matter what culture we are from, everyone loves music."

It is at times like that, that we are neither Russians, Syrians, or Americans, but just human beings who feel loss, and genuinely wish peace and happiness towards one another. With a little help from my friend who has tutored me, I'm going to try to convey those thoughts in Russian, so please bear with me:

[Our love and prayers are with you. God bless you.]

Thank you all for coming. Now Diane Sare will say something. She is the director of the Schiller Institute New York City Chorus.

Diane Sare: Thank you very much. I would also like to thank the New York Police Department, the Bayonne Fire Department, and all of those who are joined together in the fight to save human beings, as Captain Haiber said, and to protect people against terrorism, and people who responded and gave their lives on September 11.

I am going to read a statement from Col. Richard Black, State Senator of Virginia's 13th District.

Statement of Col. Richard Black: Today, the civilized world stops to give thanks to Almighty God for the Alexandrov Ensemble, its musicians, its dancers, and the journalists and beloved charity worker who perished on a flight to Syria on December 25, 2016.

At a time when many nations engaged in a sinister conspiracy to unleash hideous terror on the peaceful Syrian people, Russia boldly stepped forth, and its armed forces fought heroically alongside Syrian forces. Together, they conquered ISIS and restored peace and safety to a beleaguered people.

Just as the Russian Armed Forces brought security and freedom to millions of Syrians, the Alexandrov Ensemble came to bring precious gifts of civilization, morality and decency to that heroic land.

The Alexandrov Ensemble symbolized Russia's commitment to preserving civilization from powerful forces of evil. Beautiful strains of classical music still haunt the ruins of Palmyra, recalling Russia's and Syria's recapture of the priceless ruins from terrorists sent by foreign powers to ruin, loot, and desecrate the archeological legacy of all mankind.

I would like to express my deepest gratitude to Russia and to President Vladimir Putin for rescuing Syria from terrorists sent by foreign powers to rape, behead, crucify and degrade every decent human in Syria. I thank you for sending your finest artists—the Alexandrov Ensemble—as a clear demonstration that Russia does not wish to bring war, but rather to bring peace, beauty and God's blessings upon mankind.

My prayers are with Russia, the Alexandrov Ensemble, and all who fight to defend freedom in Syria.

May God bless you all.

Captain Haiber: Thank you Diane. Now we're going to move the wreath over to the monument. We'd ask everyone to take a flower and place it at the wreath.

Once again, thank you all for coming. And now, as we leave, please feel free to stop by the firehouse and have some coffee and everyone can warm up. Thank you once again, and God bless.

Observers, choristers, and officials alike expressed their happy realization of the importance of what they

Schiller Institute Chorus singing Russian and U.S. national anthems.

were involved in, through this anniversary commemoration occurring on Russian Orthodox Christmas Eve (Epiphany in the Western Christian calendar).

One commented: "The sense that I had, was that the people who spoke were just so genuine. You see so many of these memorials, and people are just reading a speech, or mumbling into the microphone, but I was crying throughout the whole thing. It was really, really moving to have people from three different nations come together and honor an ensemble that I never experienced live. But it was just the fact that they were [being honored]. We were there as human beings to honor and recognize the role that Beauty plays in the relationship among the world's people." Captain Don Haiber, speaking to members of the media present, said "I've learned through the Schiller Institute and through the Alexandrov Ensemble that music might be the place where we can all be brought together."

The unity of intention and of moral effect achieved by the ceremony was not contrived. An uncanny occurrence, over coffee and donuts immediately following the outdoor ceremony, illustrates the deeper, real connection that had long antedated the simple occasion of the memorial. VIPS founder Ray McGovern was a Russia analyst for the CIA from 1963 to 1990. Initially

seeking to warm up the still-freezing group with a joke, he wondered aloud, "Why didn't my good friend Vladimir Putin tell me this monument was here, and that he came here in 2005 to dedicate it?" He said the Tear Drop Memorial, which he had just discovered that day, was a profound offering of love and respect to the American people.

Captain Haiber also spoke of the significance for Americans of the memorial, which contains the names of all those known to have perished in the September 11 attack. (Terry Strada, founder of 9/11 Families and Victims United in the Struggle Against Terrorism, whose deceased husband Tom Strada's name is written on the monument, was unable to attend as she had last year, but sent this short message: "Please let them know that as long as their names are always spoken and their stories are kept alive, they will never be forgotten.")

McGovern then recited in Russian a passage from the poem, "Paying Attention to the Horrors of War," by Nikolai Nekrasov, which he had used for his talk at the Moscow commemoration of the 70th anniversary of the meeting of Russian and American forces on the Elbe, on April 25, 1945, two weeks before VE day.

He asked the group, "How many Americans know

what the Russians went through at the end of the Second World War? How many know that the Russians lost 27 million people, and the United States lost 500,000? This is not about "numbers," but the magnitude of what that represents for a population. What, for example, does this mean for Putin, who lost his oldest brother in that war? I lost my older brother from spinal meningitis, and that was very difficult for me. Imagine losing your brother from a war, and then imagine a whole nation of people like that. Therefore, for people to remember, and for people to know—that is the significance of why we were there today."

McGovern concluded his extempore thoughts by referring to the famous picture of the Americans and Russians meeting at the Elbe River in April of 1945. "That's the end of the war. That was more significant than Normandy, in a sense," he said. Father John Fencik, who had been speaking to others about his boyhood in Chicago, added, "You know, my uncle was at Elbe. He was the translator for the American and Russian troops there!"

The Concert

Later that afternoon, an extraordinary concert was held at Good Shepherd-Faith Presbyterian Church in Manhattan. In the audience were three individuals who had lost immediate family members in the Tu-154 crash. Dr. Zatsepina, whose speech I quoted at the opening of this article, concluded her remarks as follows (excerpted).

Dr. Olga Zatsepina: In the list of the passengers who didn't survive on that tragic day, a year ago, is the name of Anton Gubankov.

His mother, Marianna Viktorovna Proshkina, and his sister, Liza Kaymin-Gubankova, are in the audience with us today. We express our deep condolences for your loss.

We are dedicating this concert, prepared by the Chorus of the Schiller Institute, to the memory of the legendary Alexandrov Ensemble and all people who died on December 25, 2016 in that plane, and to the memory of your son, Anton Gubankov.

Anton Gubankov served as the Director of the newly organized Department of Culture at the Russian Defense Ministry.

Anton was born on January 29, 1965 in Leningrad. His father, Nikolay Gubankov, was a professor of Philosophy in the Theater Academy, and his mother, Marianna Proshkina, is an artist-painter. Anton came from a very famous Russian artistic family of painters who were apprentices in the workshop of Petrov-Vodkin. Their paintings are exhibited in the Russian State Museum today.

Anton Gubankov graduated from the Philology department of Leningrad State University, majoring in the French language. After graduation he worked for three years in Syria, teaching the Russian language in Homs, a city which is completely ruined today.

A true renaissance man, he collected antique books, knew several foreign languages: French, Arabic and English.

Later, at the reception, we learned that another member of the audience had lost his brother on that flight as well.

Following Dr. Zatsepina's speech, I again read Senator Black's statement and also read the short message of condolence from Rev. Andrew Ashdown in Britain, an Anglican priest who has traveled to Syria a number of times since the conflict began, and returned to report the truth about the war, in England and elsewhere. His meeting with Syrian President Bashar Al-Assad and his dissent from the official British policy toward Syria, have earned him a barrage of criticism, including from the BBC, but it has not muted his voice.

Message from Rev. Andrew Ashdown: I write to convey my sincere condolences on the anniversary of the loss of the Alexandrov Ensemble last year, as they were travelling to bring light and joy to the people of Syria at Christmas 2016. It was a time of new hope following the liberation of the city of Aleppo, which I was privileged to witness first hand, and that hope continues to shine as the terrorists are defeated all over the country, and as the people of Syria begin already to embark upon the rebuilding of their great country. Syrians are a beacon of resilience, faith and determination in the face of so much violence, and Russia has been a great blessing in helping to ensure the survival of the Syrian nation, and the possibility of peace. We thank God for all those who have given their lives in the service of the Syrian people, and especially today, those who through music and culture, celebrate and witness to the life we have in common. May those who died in order to share that vision, rest in peace.

Following these remarks, and knowing that bereaved family members of those who died last Christmas were seated in the audience, the musicians were profoundly moved, and this was evident in their impassioned performance.

The young violinist XinOu David Wei whispered to these family members before he began to play, saying "I hope that Bach will help them to rest in peace." He performed the Bach Chaconne in D minor to open the program, in resonance with the May 2016 concert, "Prayer for Palmyra: Music Revives Ancient Ruins," of the Mariinsky Theatre Orchestra, held in the famous ruins of Palmyra, Syria which had been desecrated by ISIS' acts of terror. Not a whisper was heard as the audience sat enraptured by his playing.

Schiller Institute NYC Chorus

The quartet, accommpanied by Saffron Chung, singing at the One-year Memorial Musical Commemoration, Jan. 6, 2017 in New York City. From left to right: Indira Mahajan, Linda Childs, John Sigerson, and Costas Tsourakis.

He was followed by soprano Michelle Fuchs, who sang very sweetly a Russian folk song, particularly appreciated by Russian speakers in the audience. She was accompanied by Kimmy Szeto, a very capable pianist, who has a lively commitment to music as part of life. This was his first time working with the Schiller Institute, and he seemed very happy about it.

Bass-baritone Costas Tsourakis, who sang in the Mozart Requiem performances on the fifteenth anniversary of 9/11 in 2016, sang "Lord God of Abraham" from Mendelssohn's *Elijah*, followed by soprano Indira Mahajan, who sang the Bach/Gounod "Ave Maria." Both were accompanied by pianist Saffron Chung; again, the performances were very beautifully done, solid and musical, and inspired by the occasion, and inspiring the audience.

The "Recordare" from Mozart's Requiem, with Indira Mahajan, soprano; Linda Childs, alto; John Sigerson, tenor; Costas Tsourakis, bass-baritone; and Saffron Chung on the piano, was exquisite. The balance was excellent, and each musician seemed to understand and mean what she or he was singing:

Remember, dear Jesus,
That I am the reason for Thy journey [into this world]:
Do not cast me away [from Thee] on that day.
Seeking me, Thou didst sit down weary,

Thou didst redeem me, suffering the death on the
　Cross:
Let not such toil have been in vain.

Just Judge of vengeance,
Grant me the gift of pardon
Before the day of reckoning.

I groan like one condemned:
My face blushes for my sins:
Spare a supplicant, O God.

Thou who didst absolve Mary [Magdalene],
And heard the robber,
Hast given me hope as well.

My prayers are not worthy:
But Thou, of Thy goodness, deal generously [with me],
That I burn not in the everlasting fire.

Give me a place among the sheep,
And separate me from the goats,
Setting me on Thy right hand.

The chorus performed two pieces *a capella*, directed by John Sigerson and myself, respectively. The first was "Praise the Name of the Lord" from *All Night Vigil*, by Russian composer Alexander Grechaninov, and William Dawson's arrangement of "Soon-ah Will Be Done."

Finally, alto Linda Childs, joined by Margaret

Greenspan on the piano, closed the program with the first and last of Brahms' *Four Serious Songs*. They were powerfully rendered, and the full meaning of their profound words was apparent.

1. From Ecclesiastes 3:19-22

For that which befalleth the sons of men befalleth beasts;
even one thing befalleth them:
as the one dieth, so dieth the other;
yea, they have all one breath;
so that a man hath no preeminence above a beast:
for all is vanity.

All go unto one place;
all are of the dust,
and all turn to dust again.

Who knoweth the spirit of man that goeth upward,
and the spirit of the beast that goeth downward to the earth?

Wherefore I perceive that there is nothing better,
than that a man should rejoice in his own works;
for that is his portion;
for who shall bring him
to see what shall be after him?

4. From I Corinthians 13:1-3, 12-13
Though I speak with the tongues of men and angels,
and have not agape,
I am become as sounding brass,
or a tinkling cymbal.

And though I have the gift of prophecy,
and understand all mysteries,
and all knowledge;
and though I have all faith,
so that I could remove mountains,
and have not agape,
I am nothing.

And though I bestow all of my goods to feed the poor,
and though I give my body to be burned,
and have not charity,
it profiteth me nothing....

For now we see through a glass darkly;
but then face to face;

now I know in part;
but then shall I know
even as I am known.

And now abideth faith, hope, love, these three;
but the greatest of these is love.

After the concert, a lively reception was held in the slightly warmer social hall downstairs. Everyone was invited to sing all three verses of the Russian National Anthem, which was done with gusto. The audience was a wonderful combination of Russians, Chinese-Americans from the Schiller Institute Chorus, and friends of the musicians and chorus.

As Captain Haiber said at the Tear Drop ceremony, Americans seem to be desperately seeking beauty and affirmation of our dignified human nature. After all, although the potential for the United States to enter a new paradigm of peace and prosperity, based on President Trump's stated intent to work with Russia and China, is undeniable, the vicious barrage of pornographic and violent media attacks on that potential, creates fear and uncertainty, and the future of the United States, and the world, is not secure.

Appropriately enough, while we spent the weekend of Orthodox Christmas reflecting on the important legacy of the Alexandrov Ensemble, and the urgent need for the United States to leave the realm of geopolitics forever, the reconstituted Alexandrov Ensemble was in China for several days of glorious, inspiring performances, doing the tour they were to have done a year ago. This concert tour fulfills what Helga Zepp-LaRouche called for in the last paragraph of her message of condolence a year ago:

"There is a New Paradigm in the process of becoming, as exemplified by the integration of the Eurasian Union and the New Silk Road Initiative, establishing a completely new kind of relations among nations. We need a dialogue of the best traditions of each culture for this New Paradigm to grow into a new era of civilization—the knowledge of the best of another culture will lead to a love for it, and therefore supersede xenophobia and hatred with more noble emotions. In this new era, geopolitics will be overcome forever and the dedication to the common aims of mankind will establish a higher level of reason. It is a reason for consolation for all of us, that the tragic death of the victims of the plane crash contribute with their immortality to the building of that better world."

BARBARA BOYD TO LAROUCHE PAC IN MANHATTAN

End the Coup!

This is the author's edited version of her presentation to LaRouche PAC's Special Town Hall Meeting of Jan. 5. The meeting was titled, "End the Coup, Stop the Next War, and Build the World Land-Bridge." Boyd is the author of the Robert Mueller Dossier.

On Jan. 6, 2017, one day short of a year ago today, Barack Obama's intelligence chiefs released a document designed to up-end the Presidency of Donald Trump. It was the "assessment" by a group of hand-picked intelligence analysts tasked by then CIA Director John Brennan and Obama's Director of National Intelligence (DNI) James Clapper, that President Vladimir Putin had ordered a Russian "influence" campaign to swing the 2016 Presidential election to Donald Trump.

The centerpiece of that alleged influence campaign, the claim upon which the entirety of Russiagate rises or falls, was the assertion that the Russians hacked the Democratic National Committee and John Podesta, Hillary Clinton's campaign chairman. Emails from these alleged hacks were publicly released showing that Clinton and the DNC were rigging the Democratic primaries against Bernie Sanders, and that Clinton herself was a craven puppet of Wall Street.

A secondary claim in the "assessment," and much elaborated in subsequent televised hearings before Congress, is the notion that Vladimir Putin is a master of propaganda. According to this claim, Putin can bend your mind like the worst James Bond villain if you give

Barbara Boyd

him a Facebook account and a few dollars. For a dime, he can literally suck out souls using social media even while others spend a billion dollars more on the same social media to no apparent effect.

Tonight I believe we will show you that this "assessment" is a lie, a very dangerous one, which has launched our nation and humanity on a path toward World War III.

Little noticed in the sensationally covered Jan. 6, 2017 "intelligence assessment," was a note stating that the primary source for this information was British intelligence. This fact was described as "closely held" in the *New York Times* story of Jan. 6. It was bragged about in a London *Guardian* article of Jan. 7. The *Guardian* story notes: "Over the course of the campaign, British officials were as alarmed as their U.S. counterparts over the extent of contacts between Trump advisers and Moscow and by Trump's consistently pro-Russian stance on a range of foreign policy issues." That quote is worth repeating. That is the actual strategic issue in Russiagate, the reason this nation's elites appear to have gone progressively mad, and seem more unhinged with each passing day. On Jan. 23, 2017, two weeks after the British role in the Russian hack story was leaked to the *New York Times*, Robert Hannigan, the head of the British signals intelligence agency known as GCHQ, suddenly and unexpectedly resigned.

According to the *Times* story and the factless "assessment" circulated by some in our intelligence com-

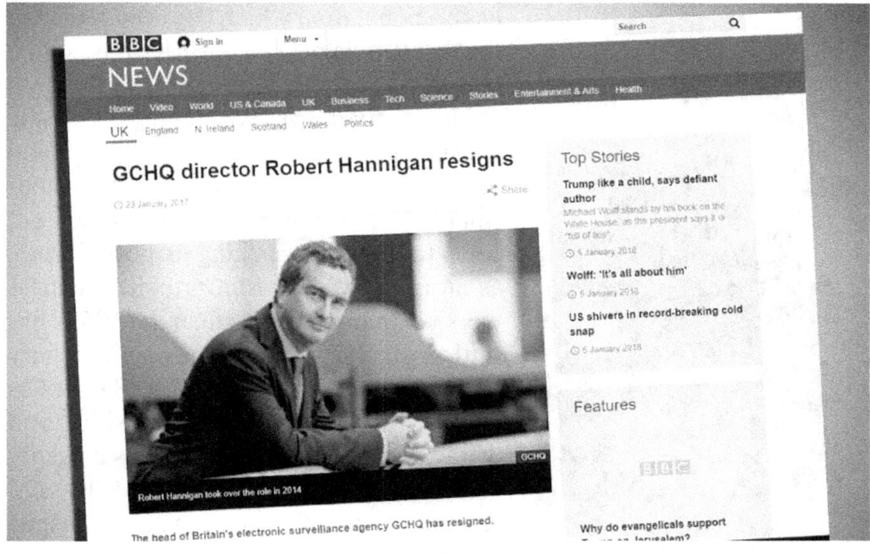

munity, the Russians gained access to DNC computers in July 2015, and the British picked it up and relayed it to the FBI and other American agencies in Autumn of 2015. As this account goes, the FBI immediately warned the DNC way back in Autumn of 2015, not once, but twice, that they had been hacked by the Russians. Absolutely nothing came of it. Instead, the DNC says that in April 2016, almost a year after the FBI warnings, the DNC noticed suspicious activity. This official account should alarm you. Could it possibly be true that the FBI tells a U.S. political party, in the midst of a presidential campaign year, that it has been hacked by the Russians, and absolutely nothing is done? In June 2016, the computer security firm CrowdStrike, hired by the Perkins Coie law-firm for the DNC, told the world that the DNC had been hacked and that the Russians did it. CrowdStrike's leading light, Dmitri Alperowitz, is a Putin-hating Russian expat otherwise working with the Atlantic Council and NATO in an active-measures campaign against the Russian state.

By July 19, 2016, former MI6 agent Christopher Steele was alleging in intelligence reports paid for by the Democratic National Committee and Hillary Clinton, that as a result of long term cultivation of Donald Trump by Russian intelligence, the DNC had been hacked to Trump's benefit, and that Russian intelligence worked directly with Trump on this operation and on other operations to secure Trump's victory in the 2016 elections. In return, the Steele memo of July 19 says, Trump agreed to sideline Ukraine as a campaign issue and to provide Putin with information on Russian oligarchs living in the U.S.A.

Steele had worked extensively with James Comey's FBI and the CIA in the past. His reports, paid for by Hillary Clinton and the DNC through the same Perkins Coie law-firm that paid for CrowdStrike's Russian hacking analysis, were delivered to both the FBI and CIA. We now know that the wife of Bruce Ohr, a high ranking Justice Department official, worked on the Russiagate project for Steele's longtime U.S. business partner, Fusion GPS. Steele had unauthorized meetings with Bruce Ohr.

In July 2016, the FBI opened an unprecedented counterintelligence investigation of a U.S. political candidate, Donald Trump, based on information delivered to it from a foreign country, namely Great Britain. FBI Director Comey admitted that the salacious British allegations against Trump were unvetted, unproven, and unverifiable. Yet it appears that Obama and his intelligence chiefs obtained surveillance warrants from the FISA Court, and, much more importantly, utilized the awesome surveillance and dirty tricks potentials of Executive Order (E.O.) 12333 against Trump and his campaign. E.O. 12333, which Bill Binney can tell you more about, aims at "neutralizing" a foreign adversary, and is the rubric under which most U.S. surveillance is conducted. This time, the full power of that weapon was used to target an American political campaign. Additionally, it appears that Obama's intelligence services actively helped Hillary's campaign by allowing her campaign to proceed with the unchallenged assertion, throughout the last stretch of the presidential campaign, that government agencies were seriously investigating whether Donald Trump was Putin's Manchurian candidate. The same agencies knew all along that the British claims were trash and that Hillary Clinton paid for them. Peter Strzok, the FBI counterintelligence official leading the FBI counterintelligence operation against Trump, appears to have talked about the Russiagate investigation as an "insurance policy" against the possibility of Trump's election with Andy McCabe, James Comey's Deputy FBI Director.

Today, Senators Lindsay Graham and Charles Grassley called for a criminal investigation of Christopher Steele for lying to the FBI about how his memos against Donald Trump were published by him during

Director of National Intelligence James Clapper (right) talks with President Barack Obama in the Oval Office, with John Brennan and other national security aides present.

the course of the 2016 campaign. Through the unyielding efforts of House Intelligence Committee Chairman Devin Nunes, that Committee will now receive Justice Department documents tracking exactly how the British Steele dossier was used by the Justice Department. Yesterday, U.S. District Judge Richard Leon ordered that Fusion GPS's bank records concerning journalists it may have paid in its campaign against Trump, must be turned over to the House Intelligence Committee.

But, the net of criminal activity in this operation stretches far beyond the FBI and the Justice Department. It included the Obama White House and most certainly John Brennan and James Clapper. I saw an interview with Bill Binney the other day, where he said the only thing which will make these people stop is for them to go to jail for their crimes against our Republic. I fully concur with that statement. The question is, can we mobilize the public hard and fast enough to make this happen in time?

It has been a very long and tumultuous year in the history of our Republic, and the future is not secured. We have a population which has been fed a big lie, that Russia hacked the elections. While partisans on both sides of this fight do battle, everyone in Washington with the possible exception of Donald Trump, and the people addressing you tonight, and our small associated army of truth-seekers, accepts the Russian hacking as gospel truth, as an act of war. A McCarthyite sickness worse in many respects than the 1950s has settled in, and war is, once again, solidly on the agenda. The media acts like an Orwellian Ministry of Truth, punishing and ostracizing anyone who questions the daily diet of "Resist!" and "Russia! Russia! Russia!" as a right-wing fanatical conspiracy theorist. Similar lies about Chinese manipulations of our body politic and of our economy are beginning to appear with regularity.

Where Do We Go from Here?

You can't really correct this mess unless you provide the population with a full understanding of why it is happening. People talk about the "Deep State." I insist that that's really a misnomer. What we are talking about is the last throes of the Anglo-Dutch monetary and political system put into place immediately after the Second World War, but drawing its assumptions about the world and about relations between nation states from the early 20th Century nostrums of British geopolitician Lord Halford Mackinder. Under Mac-

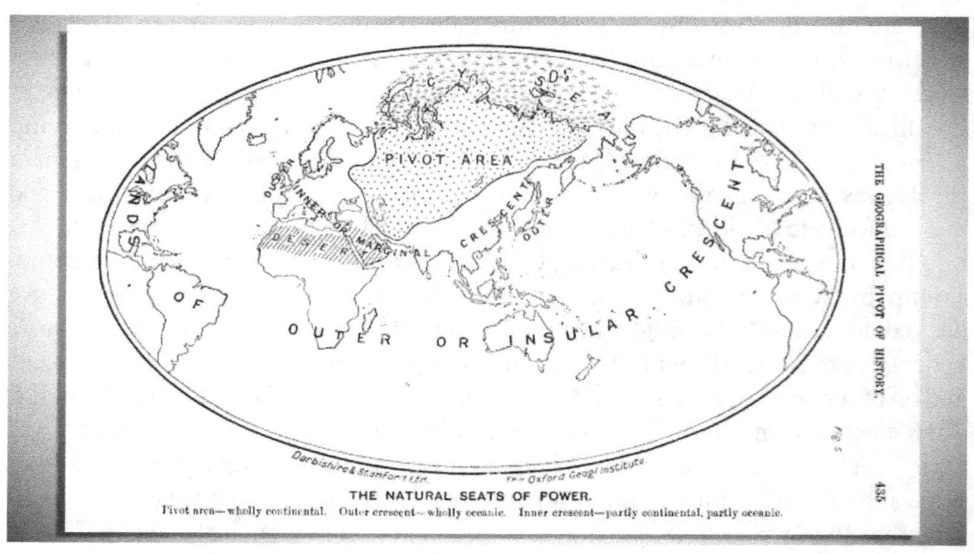

THE NATURAL SEATS OF POWER.
Pivot area—wholly continental.   Outer crescent—wholly oceanic.   Inner crescent—partly continental, partly oceanic.

kinder's theory, which has been the hegemonic idea of all British imperial policy from his time forward, "Who rules East Europe commands the Heartland; Who rules the Heartland commands the World Island; Who rules the World Island commands the World." [See Mackinder's map, p. 34.] Henry Kissinger and Zbigniew Brzezinski, the authors of so much American genocide and the current theorists of the Washington foreign policy elites, are Mackinder devotees—geopolitical fanatics. So was the Nazi theorist Karl Haushofer.

Since 2013, China has embarked on a grand initiative called the "One Belt, One Road" project. In conjunction with Russia, Eurasia—Mackinder's geopolitical pivot for the world—will be crisis-crossed with high speed rail and with whole new cities, and its infrastructure and populations fully developed. To our current establishment, this is a geopolitical nightmare, an existential threat. They need to control Russia, hopefully to continue looting it as they did in the 90s, and to control the developing world in order to sustain their post-World War II imperial model.

Barack Obama responded to China's initiative not by joining it, as President Xi offered, but by overthrowing the government of Ukraine and attempting to surround and thwart China via the Trans-Pacific Partnership (TPP) and naval encirclement in the Pacific. Obama was a full believer in the British "Great Game" and in the Thucydides trap, the theory which claims that the rise of China dictates that the Anglo-Americans must go to war. Obama had set the nation on a path to war which Hillary Clinton was supposed to complete.

China proposes an end to geopolitics by engaging in what it calls "win-win" cooperation, where nations identify common aims, such as the conquest of poverty, and work to achieve that goal, while respecting the social systems of participating nation states.

So, as Obama and Hillary Clinton prepared for war, along came Donald Trump who said we should get along with Putin. Along came Donald Trump saying he will be best friends with Xi Jinping. Trump even talks about the U.S.A. participating in the Belt and Road Initiative, which would create thousands of productive jobs here. Along came Donald Trump talking about withdrawing the United States from this whole Mackinderite perpetual warfare show. Trump's campaign and election represented a deadly threat to the Anglo-Americans. He, in effect, stopped a war which had already been set into motion—and now the Anglo-Americans are frantically attempting to re-establish that course. That is really what is going on behind the day-to-day media show. This is the actual clash behind the curtain. And I have to ask—who do you think is more sane?

I really don't think my emphasis on the British here is subject to question. Here is the preface to Peter Wright's famous exposé of MI5 and MI6, *Spycatcher*, which was written in 1988: "John LeCarré once wrote that the British Secret Services have an image but no face. It is an image which

> "John LeCarre once wrote that the British Secret Services have an image but no face. It is an image which has been carefully cultivated since they were founded in the first decade of the twentieth century. The CIA may have greater resources, the KGB greater machinations, Mossad the greater ruthlessness,
>
> *- Peter Wright, Spycatcher 1988*

> "but MI5 and MI6 were the first players in Kipling's Great Game; they are its master craftsmen. They invented the principles of tradecraft, they broke the first codes, ran the best agents, bred the best spymasters, and taught the rest everything they know. Above all, they keep the secrets.
>
> *- Peter Wright, Spycatcher 1988*

> "In the intelligence world MI5 and MI6 are still primes inter pares . . . the spy world remains the last arena where wellborn Englishmen can still exercise that effortless superiority which for centuries they were born to believe was theirs by right."
>
> *- Peter Wright, Spycatcher 1988*

has been carefully cultivated since they were founded in the first decade of the Twentieth Century. The CIA may have greater resources, the KGB greater machinations, Mossad the greater ruthlessness, but MI5 and MI6 were the first players in Rudyard Kipling's Great Game; they are its master craftsmen. They invented the principles of tradecraft, they broke the first codes, ran the best agents, bred the best spymasters, and taught the rest everything they know. Above all, they keep the secrets. In the intelligence world MI5 and MI6 are still *primus inter pares*.... The spy world remains the last arena where wellborn Englishmen can still exercise that effortless superiority which for centuries they were born to believe was theirs by right."

Just look at the British pedigree of the main players in Russiagate to date. There is the British origin of the Russia-hack myth. There are Christopher Steele and his MI6 friends. British intelligence has, through NATO and on its own, run a huge active-measures propaganda operation against Russia ever since the war on Ukraine, specifically seeking to delegitimize any favorable view of Putin or Russia. Christopher Steele played a major role in the British/Obama Ukraine coup, writing hundreds of memos to Assistant Secretary of State for European and Asian Affairs Victoria Nuland and Secretary of State John Kerry, and using the same sources, he says, that he used in his salacious attacks on Trump. Part of this British propaganda operation was running at the Democratic National Committee in 2016, using official Ukrainian and other East Bloc intelligence resources to attack Trump campaign manager Paul Manafort and candidate Donald Trump. Academics from this British/NATO propaganda campaign have provided most of the "evidence" to our Congress concerning Russian social media practices and alleged crimes.

Who provided the allegedly incriminating emails about the now-infamous meeting at Trump Tower with the Russian lawyer? It was the weird British publicist Rob Goldstone. Where is the guy I call Baby George Papadopoulos working, while he showers the Trump campaign with emails trying to set up meetings with Putin? He is working for a company called Energy Stream in London, which is working on the so-called Southern Gas Corridor designed to destroy Russian natural gas hegemony in sections of Europe. What is the relationship between Fusion GPS and Christopher Steele's Orbis? As Steele described it to Luke Harding, his recent public relations man, they provide dirt to all sides in the various wars between Russian oligarchs—a perfectly designed British penetration operation, were you to ask me. Who misdirects the Senate Judiciary Committee to allege that Russia, rather than the British, is ultimately responsible for the Steele dossier? Who but Bill Browder, the British intelligence asset *par excellence*? Luke Harding also informs us that the British have been keeping book on Donald Trump ever since an early visit to Russia in 1987. The British convinced themselves that the KGB made this trip happen.

I am sure there are some points here with which my co-panelists would disagree. My intelligence credentials are hardly anywhere near theirs. I come from the school of hard knocks, coupled with a lifelong endeavor to understand and use the method and strategic analysis of Lyndon LaRouche. Like Trump, LaRouche got in big trouble with the British, challenging them directly. That resulted in a letter to the FBI in 1982 from the British government, more or less demanding LaRouche's prosecution. They claimed he was a Russian agent of influence. Robert Mueller, the man designated to take out Trump via assassination-by-legal-brief, played a key role in that prosecution together with a propaganda apparatus set up by George H.W. Bush, Bill Casey (CIA director, 1981-87), and the CIA's Walter Raymond, Jr. That apparatus constantly defamed LaRouche as an unstable maniac akin to Attila the Hun. Mueller is not an honorable Marine. He has constantly covered up the crimes of the Anglo-American elite, including the London-headquartered Bank of Credit and Commerce International (BCCI) and the Saudi murders of almost 3,000 Americans on 9/11/2001. As we document in the dossier LaRouche PAC produced on Mueller, he is like Herman Melville's Captain Ahab, and he will do his assigned task if the American people let him.

But, we agree on the most essential point that Russiagate, as portrayed, is a dangerous hoax. The whole Russiagate narrative rises or falls on the question of whether or not the Russians hacked the DNC. If that is untrue—together with the accompanying British fabrication called the Steele dossier—then the whole story falls apart, and its perpetrators are exposed to prosecution for their fabrications. Messrs. Binney and McGovern are true national heroes in exposing what they have exposed. So let's listen to them, and then let's figure out how we get this really aired with the American public.

The Russian 'Hack' Is an Obvious Fake

William E. Binney was formerly NSA (National Security Agency) Technical Director for World Geopolitical and Military Analysis, and Co-founder of NSA's Signals Intelligence Automation Research Center. He resigned from the NSA on Oct. 31, 2001, after more than 30 years with the agency. The following is an edited transcript of Binney's presentation to the special LaRouche PAC Manhattan Town Hall Meeting of Jan 5.

William Binney: Thank you. I'd like to make a comment about some of the British intelligence and how they were the "experts of the world." That was true was a lot of fun, you could figure out all the things they had in their secret safes and envelopes inside the safes, things they didn't even know they had. But I could figure that out, and it was pretty straightforward and easy. Unfortunately, there were not too many people at NSA who understood or wanted to follow that process. That means there's nobody there knowing or doing that kind of thing any more, and it's why they were surprised when the Russians moved more troops into Crimea. That's also why they were surprised when the Russians moved into eastern Ukraine. None of that would have been a surprise to me, considering all the

Ray McGovern

William E. Binney

until about the late 50s, early 60s, and then I came to NSA. I was never impressed with anything they did. On matters concerning the Soviet Union and the Warsaw Pact—they referred to me as the "Bottom Line." So, I had the title of being the Bottom Line. I thought that was a cute title. I used to send them "woozlegrams" all the time; every time I would solve a system, I would take it through, step by step, how the solution worked and how you could figure it out, so that they could do it, too. That was part of the reason they called me the Bottom Line. That is, I figured out so many things; I figured out all kinds of secret things that nobody ever saw and didn't know about. Even the Russians didn't know they had it. But if you did the things I did, which

techniques I used and the understanding that I had of the Russian military and how they operated. And also the Russian mind, the way they think, which is very important, too, because that gives you the idea of how to solve things. So, that's a little background.

Ray McGovern: Tell us about those indicators, Bill.

The Failure of U.S. Intelligence

Binney: I had five indicators, none of which were on the U.S. indicator list. They were the real ones, the ones that had meaning, the way you could separate training from real things in the world. And I watched it happen in Czechoslovakia, the Yom Kippur War, Af-

The Coming Crash Can Be Prevented   37

ghanistan, even the Chernobyl events, even the threat to Poland. All of that surfaced with those five warning indicators, none of which were on the U.S. official list of warning indicators—so! And then, when I figured it out and laid it all out, everybody inside NSA who was involved said, "We can't tell anybody about this. We have to keep this secret." Well, that's contrary to the way I thought. I thought we should share everything, so that everybody knew how to do things, and if they could also do it, they'd get effective on a wider scale. My policy inside NSA was "share, share, share," and theirs was, "shut up, shut up, shut up."

So, "don't share, don't share, don't share." Because their policy was pretty simple; if you share knowledge that you have, what that means is that everybody's got your knowledge, and you're not special. You don't have anything up on them, so you're no longer the leader, the person that somebody looks to for the answer. You know, everybody else can get the answer, too. Well, I thought that was counterproductive.

After I got to NSA, I had a lot of fun sending out "woozlegrams" to GCHQ (the British version of the NSA). Then, I looked at—and Ray and I had been discussing this—the alleged hack, which I understood to be a fabrication from the very beginning, because, first of all, NSA wasn't telling you where the packets went, and *they would know—if they were hacked—where those packets went,* because the TCP/IP packet format gives you a way of reconstructing a data transfer session, by a number—giving a specific number to a whole series of packets that belong together. So that gives you the idea how to repackage each session. And then internally in there is the IP number of the originator, and of the terminal where the packets are supposed to go.

That's what the machines do that manage the distribution of data to the Net; that's how they pass the data around. All you need is one packet to tell where it came from and where it is going. NSA has trace route programs mapping all the packet transfers around the world. They've got hundreds of trace route packets in switches and servers all around the world. In fact, the

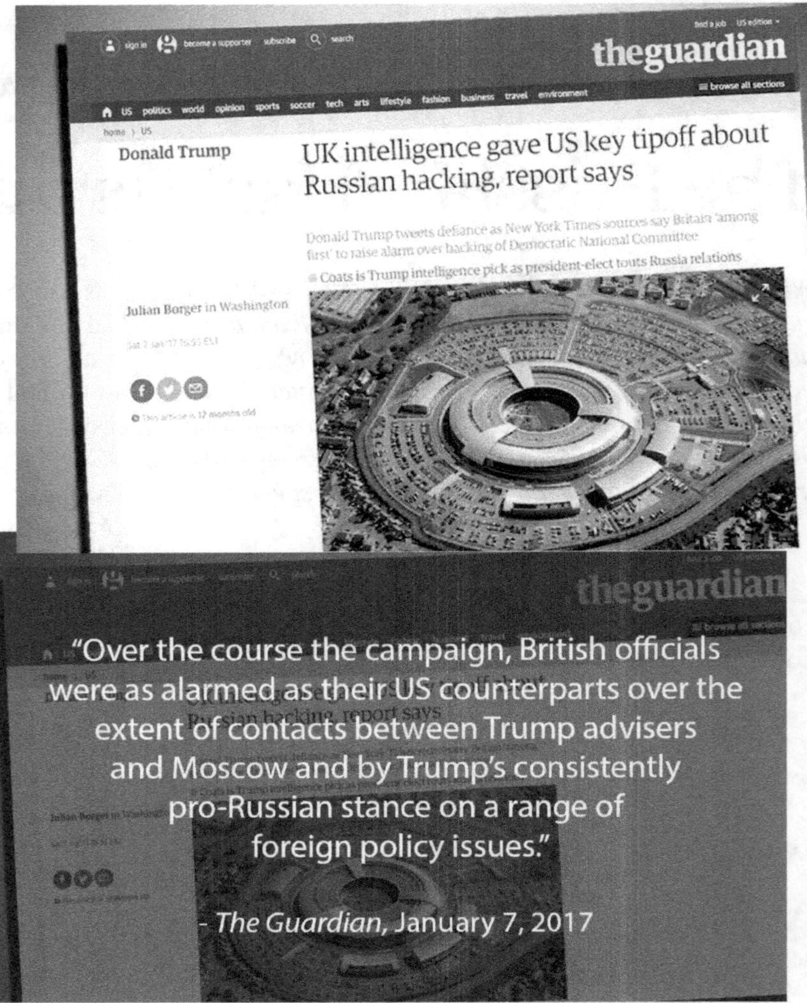

count on one of the slides released by former NSA contractor Edward Snowden shows in the computer network exploitation that the NSA had over 50,000 implants in switches and servers around the world. That means switches everywhere. The slide shows the distribution of it from the old Soviet Union, across all of Europe, through Asia, all over—and in the United States, too.

But those implants are also tied in with tapping points, where they actually use a PRISM type program, where it takes a fiber input and splits it into two and duplicates it. Then they send one to the NSA, Narus or Verint devices, depending upon whether it's AT&T or Verizon, or some other company. And then that sessionizes everything, reconstructs everything on those fiber networks, and they pass it to the storage facilities in Utah, or where-have-you—that's where they're storing all this data. My estimate of the storage facility in Utah was that it could hold 5 zettabytes of data, which is 5x10 to the 21st power bytes.

McGovern: That's a lot!

The Surveillance State

Binney: Yes it is. In fact, it's probably something like 100 times the total knowledge of everything man has ever created. But the point is, that storage facility is a million square feet, and 100,000 square feet of that is devoted to actual storage; the rest of it is power and cooling and stuff like that. But now they're planning ahead, they're planning for it to be full. If you try to collect everything—which was NSA Director General Keith Alexander's policy, he said, "let's just collect it." That means an ever increasing amount year after year. That means, year after year, you have to keep building bigger facilities to store it, because there is going to be more and more data.

They broke ground last summer for a is a 2.8 million square foot facility at Fort Meade, Md., which will be about three times the size of the one in Utah. That's the planning, to replace, once the Utah facility's full. Then they'll have that one to fill up. Because they're collecting more data every year, they need a bigger facility. And that one's probably going to cost $5-$6 billion, and it's all going to come out of our taxpayers—or else we're going to borrow it from China.

"I've been distributing information about this to all kinds of news agencies, TV, radio, and various newspapers. I've been distributing the 'Fairview at a Glance' map (**Fig. 1**) to all of these agencies, so that they could see where the tap points are inside the U.S.A. This one is for AT&T. It's called the Fairview program. If you looked at it, they keep claiming—and this is what I call the "obvious lie," the obvious lie that the American public is being told by our government—"we're only after foreigners, and that's why we have these taps and are copying all this data."

Well, if you look at this, that's distributed throughout the population centers of the United States at tap points. If the NSA only wanted foreign communications, see those green points along the coasts? There's 11 of them, on the West Coast and the East Coast. That's where all the foreign communications come through. That's where the transoceanic cables surface: All foreign communications are coming into the United States through those points, or going out from the United States, or they're transiting foreign communications coming in, going then through the U.S.A. to Canada or Mexico, or even Asia somewhere. Any transit and communication—into or out of—foreign locations, is at those green points. That's where they should be tapping if they're after foreign communications. So why do you have the rest of those tap points distributed with the population of the U.S.A.? It's because *we are the target,* that's why.

If they just want foreign communications, they have the green points already. So what's all the rest of this stuff? That's why they're building the Utah center. I, of course, was a witness at the start of this in October 2001, when they started pulling all the billing data from AT&T. It was about 400 million total average per day of long-distance calls, 320 million of those were U.S. to U.S. calls—so it was all internal to the U.S.A.

All of this was being graphed, and it was a violation of the First Amendment. Eventually the NSA could

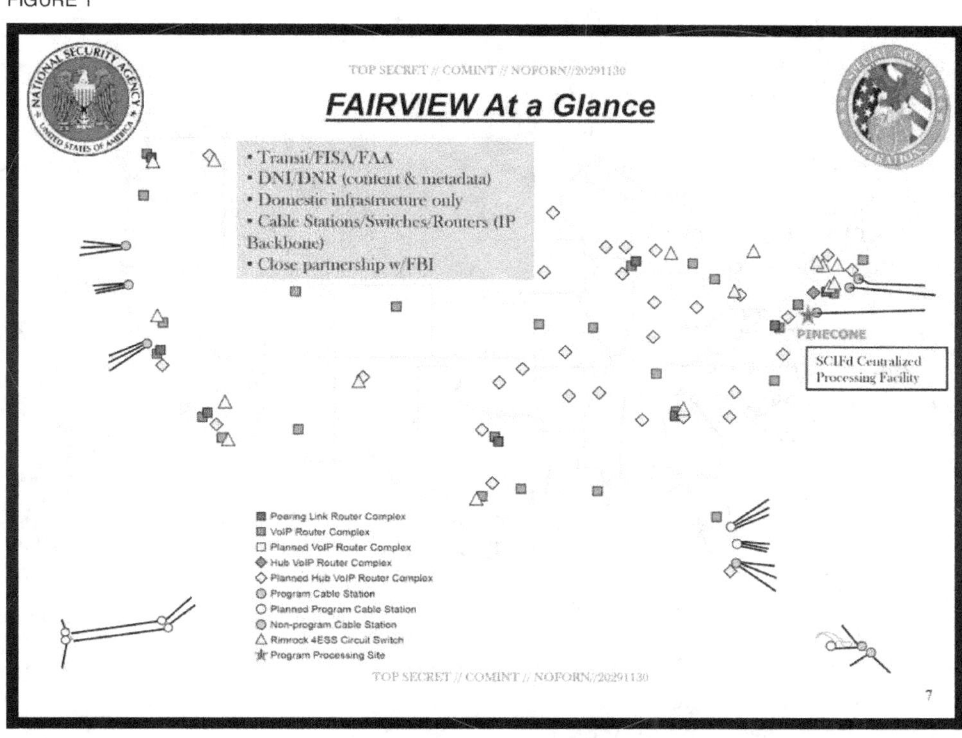

figure out a lot of things, and that would be a violation of the Fourth Amendment. Then they started using the information to prosecute people, and that was a violation of the Fifth and Sixth Amendments to the Constitution. So they kept scrapping the Constitution in doing this.

I went on the Web, using Google, and looked at this. I decided I was going to go find out where these points are. So I now have the locations of all of them, down to the building and address. I've shared this with any number of people; I gave it to the documentary film producer Laura Poitras, if she wanted to publish it, and she in turn gave it to the *New York Times*. She told me that she gave it over to them, and they refused to publish. They said if they published it and one of those points was attacked, they would be blamed. So much for the intention of the First Amendment, to have a free press that would inform the public of what their government's doing on their behalf. *Like, spying on them.*

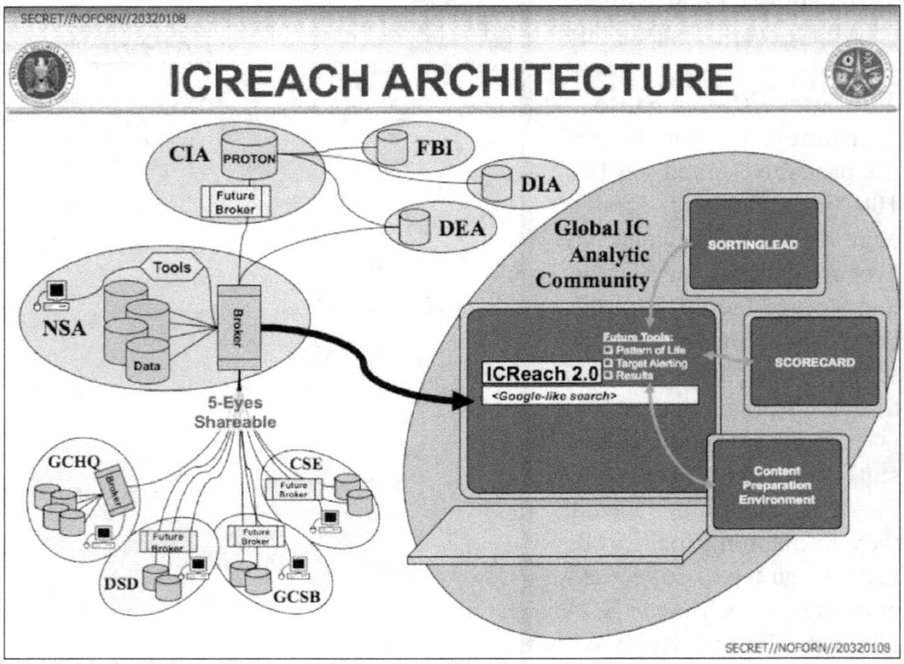

And *this is not simply metadata*; this includes all content, too. They've been lying about that from the beginning. I mean, how could you even look at something, how could you even conceive of spying on your lover to see if she or he is cheating on you—how can you do that with metadata? You have to have a *little content* to see if somebody's messin' around. OK? The point is, they had that in the NSA storage. That's a local phone call, between people locally—I mean, if you're going to have an affair you can't go too far, you know? You have to be in a reasonable proximity. [laughter]

This is what I call the "big lie," and we're all buying into this. That's why Section 702 of the Foreign Intelligence Surveillance Act (FISA) is a joke. Section 702 and oversight of it is a joke! That's not what they're doing. This is all done under Executive Order 12333, section 2.3c, where it says: If you are after a target, an international criminal or some target like militaries or things like that, or leaders of countries—like Merkel or others—it's OK to collect information and to try to find

FIGURE 2

them; that's OK, and you can store it—and oh, by the way, you can search it, too, if you want. They say, "On every fiber line, there's a probability of having a dope dealer internationally, *so let's copy them all.*" And, oh, by the way, we can keep all the data on U.S. citizens and all their communications, and we'll call it "coincidental collection," and we'll store it and interrogate it.

The Spying Apparatus

And that's what the FBI does, and that's how they get into this data. You see in the "ICREACH ARCHITECTURE" (**Fig. 2**), the CIA, FBI, DIA (Defense Intelligence Agency), DEA (Drug Enforcement Agency), and the Five Eyes (British, U.S.A., Canada, Australia, and New Zealand intelligence cooperation). This slide is from 2007, I believe. What they do is stamp the date for the first classification review, which is 25 years. So it's 2032, Jan. 8, I think. So if you subtract 25 from that, that means the slide was constructed on Jan. 8 of 2007, and the first review is 25 years later. This was the status in 2007, ten years ago. But of course, it's expanded since then; they've now got nine other countries participating with them in this program, but they access this data through a separate program called XKeyscore. And that one restricts access. In other words, these different programs have different access rules, called "rules tables," of what you're allowed to look at or interrogate or search. That's how you limit what people can do in your data base.

There are limits to some of this even in ICREACH [The NSA's top-secret surveillance-related search engine], but they can simply modify their "rules table" and they can get into everything. So that's the Five Eyes [British, U.S.A., Canadian, Australian and New Zealand intelligence], looking at all the data that the NSA has on everybody, including us and including British citizens, as well as all the others around the world. Each can spy on the other, and cooperate that way, too. It's easy; the mechanisms already exist for that; that's the easy way to do it.

This all feeds into the internal NSA programs. This was where I came in. This was my design for NSA (**Fig. 3**), the whole thing: picking out, right up front, the "Trafficthief," picking out the selected targets that you knew about, and then passing it through a process where metadata gets graphed and relationships are built. We were preparing to do "two-degree separation" of selection of data from that, as a part of the process of automatically analyzing and figuring out who the new targets were, and then adding them automatically, basically taking people out of the loop. Because they did a very bad job—I mean, they were very inconsistent and variable. It's unfortunate, but that's the way the analysts were.

Then it's all indexed down to the databases—Pinwale and Nucleon—which are the Internet database in Pinwale and the phone database in Nucleon. The phone network wasn't too much of a problem—the public switched telephone network—because it was basically run by the telephone companies for NSA. The NSA wanted these selections, and the telephone companies would provide it to the NSA, including the audio. The tap points that the NSA had would also pick up all the VOIP (Voice Over Internet Protocol) audio. That was one of the main targets. The NSA felt people were using VOIP to do criminal activity. It was cheaper, too, so they didn't have to pay as much.

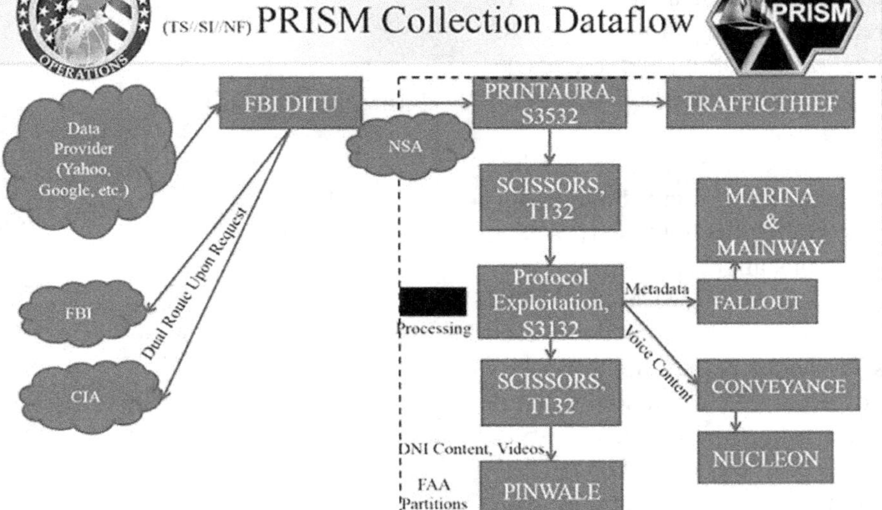

That was the entire design we left them, and they haven't changed a damned thing for 16 years. It's all been the same; there's nothing new here. This is what we left them. *Except we had several programs running that would not enable them to do what they're doing today.* Like right up front, we had programs that filtered out all data that wasn't relevant. We never took it in, so they never had the chance to abuse it. We never had to store it anywhere, because it wasn't kept there. So if you can make that decision right up front, your management of content is much easier.

That was the approach we took. But see, then Vice President Dick Cheney wanted to know—he grew up under Nixon—he wanted to know what his enemies were doing and planning, and he wanted to know what all the politicians, all his political opponents were all about. You need to know what everybody's doing to control them. So, the policy was: let's collect it all. That's really what it's all about, controlling the American population.

You can see it with the use of data against the author and reporter Jim Risen, and also against former New York Governor Eliot Spitzer—he was going after the bankers for defrauding people, fraudulent solicitations, causing the 2007-2008 crisis; he was going to go after them criminally. In order to get rid of him, they had to use the FBI, going directly in through the FBI technology center in Quantico, Virginia, directly into the NSA databases. There's no oversight of that, at all! There's no reporting of any of that, no auditing of any of it, and there's no oversight by the courts, or the Congress!

So this is what I've been telling people. They don't believe this crap? They should start asking questions about the Fairview program and all these accesses that are going on that they don't even know about, or they don't follow—or they don't *want* to know about, because if they *did* know about them, they couldn't claim plausible deniability! That's really what their action is; they can claim plausible deniability: "Oh, it didn't happen on my watch, I didn't know about that." This is the game they're playing; this is the lie they're perpetuating with us, the people. And the mainstream media are going along—*and they're worthless here!* They're basically worthless. They're all going along with this charade.

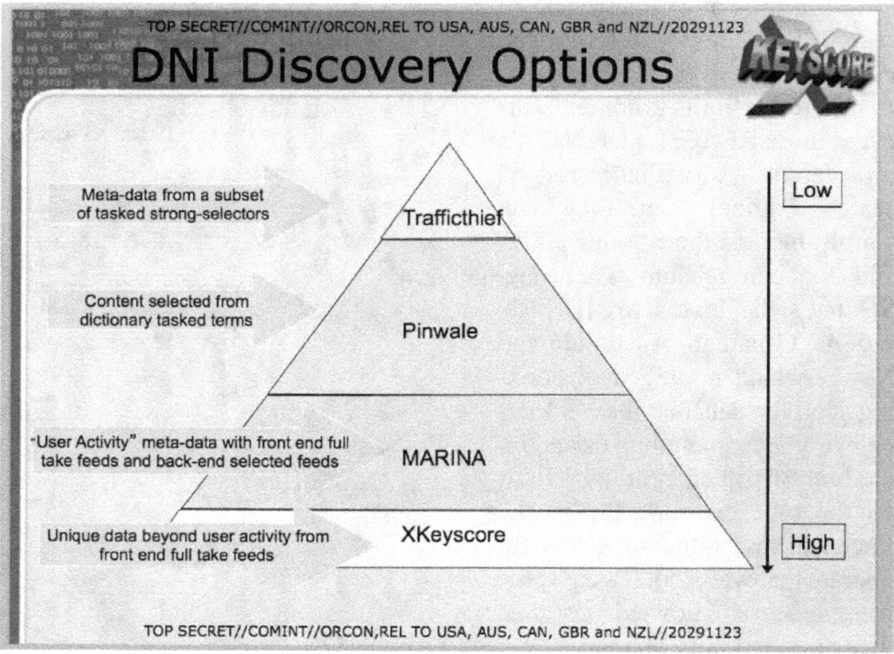

Tracing the Packets

When it came to looking at the data supposedly showing that the Russians "hacked" the DNC, here's the background: You *know* that *the NSA knows who took those packets and where they went.* All they had to do was have one packet and look internally at the TCP/IP format. They know the originator and terminating IP address, so you know where the system, the World Wide system, sent the packets. Because *they're machines,* you have to tell them exactly what to do, or it won't happen. So it's *in the format as to where the things go,* so the NSA should know who exactly got that, where that IP is.

I mean, they did it a few years ago with the Chinese. The NSA said, it came from a military building in Shanghai. So they should be able to do the same thing with any hack. And they should have packets on every hack, if they've got them. We used to see this stuff all the time. We had no problem at all finding out about it,

recognizing it—*and that was 25 years ago!* So where are they now?

That was the main reason I opposed the idea the Russians "hacked," because NSA is not saying where the packets went, *and they would know,* because they've got trace route programs in hundreds of switches all over the world, in the U.S.A. and around the world, and those switches would tell them where those packets went. They'd have captured those packets and mapped them.

All you have to do is go on the Web and do a Google search for "trace route," and it'll give you an idea of what the capability is of the commercially available versions. They also have another program called Trace-Watch, which allows you to see coming into your computer, and who's in your computer. There are various versions of that for different operating systems. So if you go on the Web and Google that, you can download it. The software is free, by the way, last time I looked. You can trace-route anybody sending you any email, you can watch who's in your computer and what they're doing.

More Intelligence Incompetence

This is the main area where all the collection accesses that NSA has, and all the data that people are feeding them to store for them. The query goes into these programs, and the indexing by the graphs of the metadata is how they pull that data out of the storage of content. Once you pick that metadata up and say, "give me all the content on this piece of metadata," the program looks at the graph and goes in and pulls out all that data. That's how they're doing retroactive research on stored data.

That's how they're doing it. And, this is the fundamental principle (**Fig. 4**), and this is why I say these people have totally lost it, they're totally incompetent. They start at the top; it says, a low possibility of discovery of new options (at the top with the Trafficthief). That's where you're working with something that's known, and even if those known things communicate with other unknowns, they ignore that because that has a really low probability of discovery. That was really our main approach, targeted, focused approach.

And then they go down to the next one, they're going into the Pinwale system. Now, going into the Pinwale system, they use the XKeyscore and ICREACH programs, which basically do dictionary select—meaning that you feed them a bunch of words or phrases, and it pulls all the data out that has any of those words or phrases in it. Which is really a dump, it's like a Google dump. So you get 50,000, up to a million, returns, and if your input is a few billion items every day, and you do a Google search through it, like that, you'll get a couple million outputs every day. Each analyst with their Google output is trying to go through this tens of thousands or millions, or hundreds of thousands of items, and they never get through. That's why they fail.

So they can't see anything coming. Then all the terrorist attacks happen, people die—"go clean up the blood in the street"—and then you find out who did it, and then you go into the database and you say, "give me all the data on this person; I know who did it, and I can do a good forensic job for the police." Which means that the intelligence community that we have—and the GCHQ and all of them—have lost the ability to do the function of intelligence, which is to predict intentions and capabilities of potential adversaries—*in advance!* So you could do something to stop it!

That was the whole idea: We wanted to stop terrorist attacks. That's why we wanted to go to 18 sites that produced information on terrorists in January 2001, and they refused to do that. So we couldn't put it against the terrorist problem, which we put as the main problem.

At any rate, this whole pyramid says the further down you go, into Marina, which is the voice side of it, and then you use XKeyscore against all the databases, so now you're going into this massive database, your data polls, based on dictionary selection, phrase selects like that, is coming out—it's getting larger and larger, and they call it "high discovery." I call that "low."

The entire thing is reversed: low is high, and high is low, but these idiots don't know what is high and low! That's why they're failing: They don't even know they're failing. I'm just a country boy from Pennsylvania, I'm from the farmlands and the mines and so on. We used to say out there, if you're failing and continuously failing, you must be doing something wrong. And if you're doing something wrong, you need to look at your whole process and figure out what you're doing wrong and fix it!

They can't even admit they have something wrong. Because it means they have a wart on their record, and so, we can't admit a wart. That's why, if there's any whistleblower, we have to step on them. That's the way they're operating: They're like alcoholics—but they can't admit they're alcoholics, so they'll never fix their problems. So all these problems continue with U.S. intelligence.

Until we step up to this, people are going to continue to die to keep this entire stupid process going. That's the problem I see. That's why I'm calling them idiots and fools for doing what they're doing. And they're doing it at the expense of the lives of people in countries around the world—not just here. They're all buying into this crap. And the British also, and they're even going overboard with video. But we're catching up, just like we're trying to catch up with the British in invading countries: They've still invaded more countries than we have.

The Non-Existent Russian Hack

And then, when we at the Veterans Intelligence Professionals for Sanity (VIPS) looked at the raw data that was produced by Guccifer 2.0, that said this was the evidence that the "hack" on the DNC was by the Russians. We went through that data. Every time there's a file transfer or something that's transferred off a computer, a file comes out like an email, and you have a timestamp at the end of the email, when it's sent; the next email, a timestamp; the next email, a timestamp; a file, a timestamp and so on. So you get a timestamp at the end of the data transfer for each component of data.

That means you can line it all up, look at the timestamps and the difference between timestamps, and calculate the number of bits and then calculate the transfer rate.

That's exactly what we did, and when we looked at the Guccifer 2.0 data, we found the highest transfer rate was 49.1 megabytes/second. We tested data transfer rates around the world to try to see how fast we could do that; can we really do it at that rate? We said we couldn't, and we alleged that, and people took issue with that. So we said, "OK we'll test it, and see." I got some hackers in Europe to try to download a file we set up here in the U.S.A., download it across the Atlantic and into the European network; and we got some from a personal computer at 100 megabits, we got 0.8 megabytes/second, instead of 49.1 megabytes/second. And then on a DSL 200 megabit commercial line, we got 1.6 megabytes/second. And then on a data center to data center transfer from the New Jersey data center to a data center in the U.K., we got 12 megabytes/second. And we had some people try it in Belgrade, and also in Albania, and they just threw up their hands, it didn't even work—it was like running off a dial-up process. You just never get it across in time, so it was pointless to even try. The best transfer output across the network we got, was 12 megabytes/second—bytes, not bits.

That meant that even with the data, it was one-fourth the speed that was necessary. But if you pass something into the network, it adds all this housekeeping data to it, like the TCP/IP transfer format and other formats, and also data showing the transfer between segments of the line and so on, and timing and all of that. So you can do a trace route. If you re-trace the route, you see that that data goes with the packets, too. That meant that it's really close to doubling that data they have to transfer, so it means really that the transfer rate was only one-fourth to one-eighth the necessary speed of the network to transfer and make that happen.

So it was impossible. We just couldn't do it. We said, we're open to anybody that can show that that can be done, and then we'll replicate it just to be sure. That's the scientific method.

We failed to transfer it, and *there was a greater implication beyond that*. That argued, by the way, that it was a local download—wherever local was—where they did it, but it did match the thumb drive transfer rate from a computer. That did match. So it could be done on a thumb drive.

But we also looked at the data.

There were two batches of data that came out of Gu-

ccifer 2.0. One was dated the 5th of July, on the 5th of July transfer; and another was dated the 1st of September. So after we looked at that, some things looked a little suspicious. I was doing this with Duncan Campbell. He and I were looking at this the month before last. If you ignored the date and the hour, and looked only at the minute, second and millisecond, *the two files merged*. They interleaved with one another, so that it could form *one continuous file*. In other words, Guccifer 2.0 was playing with the data, and then he did a ripple change, a one-sided edit, on the hour and the date.

Fraud & Fakery

What that meant was, *all of this is a fake*. It's a fabrication! All the data that they pushed to say this was evidence of a hack, is a fake! We looked at that and said, "Hmm, who's faking this? Well, the timing of it looks like it might be somebody internally here in the U.S.A., who might have also used something like the NSA's Marble Framework program, to fake things. Which is where they go in—and I think Ray wants to say more about the Marble programs so I won't go into that too much.

You have to think about this. It's funny—this is really a poor, sloppy technical job, trying to fake a hack. *Period!* That's it. This is a fabrication from the beginning, and they're all building off this fabrication, and they have nothing else to produce in terms of evidence. The mainstream media say I'm a conspiracy theorist. The only thing they can do is throw labels at me! They have no evidence whatsoever to point to, *none!* And the stuff they point to, we've already shown is a clear fabrication and a fake!

And so, they're all, what we would call in the country, "sucking a hind tit." [laughter]—If you know what that term means. If you've ever raised cows, and a calf gets on the hind tit, they get kicked! That's the whole idea of that one. It's a good country saying.

But, we also look at them as being "chip pitchers," if you know what that is from the country. [laughter] Do I have to explain that one? Cow chips. They fall, and flatten, they dry out; they get really light, and round in shape for frisbee type throwing: So they're pitching chips. It's something that's done quite frequently in Washington, D.C., OK? And it fits right into the character of what they're doing here. This is the whole thing: This is just a fake! And it's an obvious one at that.

That's all I have to say. [applause]

THE FUTURE LIES WITH THE NEW SILK ROAD!

Whither Germany? Grand Coalition or 'Musical Chairs'

by Helga Zepp-LaRouche, Chairwoman of the German political party
Bürgerrechtsbewegung Solidarität (Büso)

This an edited translation of an article that appeared in Neue Solidarität, *Jan. 11, 2018.*

Jan. 5—The exploratory government coalition negotiations with changing participants, which have lasted for almost four months, are characterized above all else by one thing: such a blatant lack of forward-looking concepts that one must be seriously concerned about the fate of Germany. After the incompetent reaction from Merkel to the miserable CDU election result—"I do not see what I could have done differently"—a growing percentage of citizens clearly recognizes that Mrs. Merkel, with her "market-compliant" understanding of democracy, doesn't give a fig for urgent tasks for the common good. According to a recent poll by the DIMAP polling institute, she fell back to third place on the popularity scale with 52%, behind SPD Foreign Minister Sigmar Gabriel (62%) and Green Party Co-Chairman Cem Özdemir (53%). Fifty-two percent are against a new grand coalition between the CDU-CSU and the SPD, 75% want a renewal of the CDU leadership, and 67% think that Merkel has her best days behind her.

But none of the people named as potential successors to Merkel has any positive vision for the future. The same applies to the SPD, where the cockfight between Chairman Martin Schulz and former Chairman Sigmar Gabriel is just as dominant as the fear of losing more votes in a new election. And in the Christian Social Union (CSU), Alexander Dobrindt is right in saying that the 68ers marched through the institutions and secured key positions in the arts, culture, media, and politics—but that does not mean that he, as a representative of a party whose name contains the word Christian, accepts, for example, the standpoint of Pope

courtesy of James Rea

SPD Foreign Minister Sigmar Gabriel (left) and Green Party Co-Chairman Cem Özdemir (right) are leading acting Chancellor Angela Merkel of the CDU in an opinion poll, as efforts to form a coalition government drag on.

wikipedia

wikipedia/ Ralf Roletschek

Francis on the refugee question, nor that he has freed the CSU from the green ideology, which is one of the consequences of the long march of the '68ers.

What a contrast to the optimistic outlook that President Xi Jinping laid out for China, and which he reiterated in his New Year's message! Xi pointed out that just last year, another 10 million people were lifted out of poverty, 13 million jobs were created, and all Chinese have been integrated into a pension and health-care system. Xi quoted the Chinese poet Du Fu: "If only I could get tens of thousands of mansions! I would house all the poor people who would then beam with smiles." Xi reiterated China's plan to lift all its remaining people out of poverty by 2020, and to use the Silk Road Initiative to help create a world of peace and development. Together with other countries, China wants to build a beautiful future for all humanity. "We agree to work together to build a community with a shared future for mankind, so as to benefit people all over the world."

And what a contrast also to the spirit of President Putin's New Year's message, which was a heartfelt reminder of the love between parents and children, expressing thanks to all the people who work on New Year's Day, calling for forgiveness of mistakes instead of resentment, and giving love, warmth, care, and attention to others.

Obviously, given the smear campaign by the Western mainstream media, this does not match the image that most people in Germany have of the President of China or Russia. But the fact of the matter is that the countries that are cooperating with China's economic belt perspective are filled with unprecedented optimism for the future of humanity, with the "Spirit of the New Silk Road." In contrast, the political process in Berlin is like the oxygen-poor atmosphere in a cheese bell—a cheese bell, however, where the various cheeses are already extremely "mature" and exhibit a corresponding intensity of odor. One could also say it less diplomatically.

President Xi Jinping has repeatedly offered all nations, including explicitly the U.S.A. and Germany, cooperation on the New Silk Road on the basis of "win-win" cooperation. The reaction of the EU has so far been clearly negative, and that of Berlin is characterized by outdated geopolitical prejudices.

The former German Ambassador to Beijing, Michael Schäfer, in an interview with the *German Business News*, raised the suspicion that the negative attitude toward the New Silk Road and the imputation of a "hegemonic approach," are the projection of Europe's own behavior in the last century. As a former diplomat,

Children playing with bundles of worthless paper money in Germany in the 1920s. The ECB feeding the financial bubble and Germany's "black zero" is creating an even bigger crisis.

he may find it appropriate to blame such a politically incorrect view on the behavior of the last century. We do not have this obligation: the behavior of the EU and the still merely acting German government is petty, stuck in the old thinking of geopolitics (which led to two world wars in the past century), and fundamentally in opposition to German interests. If Germany continues like this, it will catapult itself onto the sidelines of historical developments and sink into insignificance— to the great detriment of the German people.

In a situation where many EU Member States feel their interests are no longer represented by the EU bureaucracy for a variety of reasons, and are drifting apart, Berlin should—rather than call for a United States of Europe as Martin Schulz has done—put the really important issues on the agenda. Insisting on adherence to the supranational agenda will only increase the resistance, because there is no "European people."

China's New Silk Road Initiative is the largest infrastructure and reconstruction program in history, which is now overcoming underdevelopment and poverty with unprecedented momentum, especially in developing countries. It has already led to a completely new strategic orientation for over 70 countries, which have not only recognized their economic advantage in win-win

The options for German economic cooperation with China are readily available, since China-to-Europe rail freight capacity is increasing.

cooperation with China, but also prefer the new model of cooperation among equally sovereign states, to the old idea of a unipolar world. All these countries—including those as diverse as ASEAN, Eastern and Central Europe, the Balkans, Southern Europe, and many Latin American and African countries, but also Japan—have recognized the opportunities inherent in this new model of international politics. Japan, for example, has invited China to cooperate on four mega-projects in Africa.

Therefore, the following issues should be given priority on the agenda of the coalition negotiations: Above all, the new government must immediately express its willingness to cooperate with China on the development of the New Silk Road. Only in this way can the dangerous terrain of geopolitics, such as is being expressed in the creation of an EU army, be abandoned and replaced by the new era of a community of destiny for humanity. And only through the expansion of the New Silk Road in the Middle East and Africa, i.e. through real economic development, can the refugee crisis be solved in a humane way.

Instead of irresponsibly supporting the Troika's (European Commission, European Central Bank, and IMF) policies in favor of the casino economy and at the expense of the common good, the negotiators must finally face the urgent need to reorganize the financial system. Since absolutely nothing was done to fix the systemic failures that led to the crash of 2007/2008, a new financial crash threatens, which would be much more dramatic than the previous one due to the massive increase in corporate and sovereign debt and the derivatives bubble. A banking system in the tradition of Roosevelt's Glass-Steagall Act must immediately be placed on the agenda, and a credit system in the tradition of the *Kreditanstalt für Wiederaufbau* (Reconstruction Finance Agency), as it worked during the period of the German economic miracle, must replace the present ECB money-printing policy.

In this way, a national infrastructure program can be funded that will end the investment backlog on roads, bridges, water management, schools, etc. which was created by former Finance Minister Schäuble's policy of *schwarze Null* ("black zero"—a federal budget that is in the black, or fully balanced) at the expense of future generations. And funds could be made available to hire competent project managers and engineers from China, who would complete the Berlin BER airport and build a high-speed railway system throughout Germany worthy of the name. With such a credit system, Germany can cooperate with the AIIB, the New Silk Road Fund, and similar institutions in joint projects with other nations in the various development programs.

China has launched a comprehensive program of national renewal at the initiative of Xi Jinping, which intends to make all layers of society aware of their 5,000-year-old culture and revive the best periods in philosophy, music, painting and poetry. If we in Germany want to achieve anything like a comparable revitalization of our culture, we must free ourselves from the counterculture that was the result of the manipulations of the Congress for Cultural Freedom, the Frankfurt School and the 1968 movement, and which has brought us today's left-liberal, "politically correct" thinking patterns.

That would actually be quite simple, because in Germany we are fortunate enough to have a large number of universal poets, thinkers, inventors, and composers—from Nicholas of Cusa, Johannes Kepler, Gottfried Wilhelm Leibniz, the Humboldts, Bernhard Riemann, Albert Einstein, and Krafft Ehricke, to Bach, Beethoven, Schubert, Schumann, Brahms, Lessing and Schiller, to name but a few. We only need to bring their works to life among our contemporaries.

So far, however, the exploratory coalition negotiations are more akin to a game of Musical Chairs involving changing seats and positions, while the *Bürgerrechtsbewegung Solidarität* (Civil Rights Movement Solidarity) is the only party that offers such solutions.

Post-Election South Africa: Close Combat Over the New Economic Paradigm

by David Cherry, R.P. Tsokolibane, and M.M. Maxongo

Do not underestimate the power of the BRICS bloc and the change in the balance of world power that it represents. Especially for Africa, BRICS represents the first major opportunity in centuries to break the grip of colonialism and post-colonial oppression for the continent. Jacob Zuma understands that, and the West is none too happy about it either.

—Gayton McKenzie,
black South African millionaire,
December 2017

Jan. 9—South Africa is the only African country with a full-set industrial economy. South Africa is crucial for the future of Africa, and the future of Africa is vital to the future of the world. No wonder, then, that South Africa is an important arena in the worldwide struggle between the British empire of money and the China-inspired drive for universal industrialization.

It was South Africa's President, Jacob Zuma, who vigorously campaigned for South Africa to be included in BRICS—the brainchild of China and Russia—and later insisted that the BRICS' New Development Bank open a branch in Johannesburg. This year, 2018, South Africa again chairs the BRICS, as it did in 2013.

Another South African, Dr. Nkosazana Dlamini-Zuma, as head of the African Union (AU), 2012-2016, took bold leadership in laying plans for the industrial and cultural development of all Africa called Agenda 2063, especially with the cooperation of China. Those plans include, for example, the development of a continent-wide network of high-speed railways, plans that are now being elaborated by a technical unit of the AU in Johannesburg. And a Chinese company has now committed itself to building a new iron and steel complex in South Africa, vital for Africa's development, and is investing $3.2 billion in this complex. No one in London or New York is interested in large investments in the basics of agro-industrial development in Africa.

The contending forces—for and against Africa's agro-industrial development—are visibly active in South Africa, and never more so than in the mid-December election within the ruling party, the African National Congress (ANC). The ANC, in power since the transition to majority rule in 1994, is divided between leaders who look to China's successful economic model—the New Economic Paradigm—and to the BRICS, to achieve major advances in infrastructural, agricultural, and industrial development, and improvements in the welfare of the entire people, on the one hand, and other leaders who suffer from a well-known

Credit: Government of South Africa/GCIS

South African President Jacob Zuma (left) and Cyril Ramaphosa, newly elected president of the ruling African National Congress party (right).

delusion. We mean the delusion that the generous, kind, and honest financiers in London and New York, and their junior counterparts in South Africa, are their friends, and wish nothing but the best for South Africa—or at least, that they are the usual victors and the source of the best patronage in the long run.

The mechanics of the ANC's elections are part of the necessary background. In the mid-December election,

Credit: CC/Szekszter

Johann Rupert, one of Ramaphosa's backers.

as reported in *EIR*'s Jan. 6 issue, the ANC elected a new president and a new, 86-person National Executive Committee (NEC), the party's ruling body. The party president then becomes its candidate for President of South Africa, in a national election that takes place a year later. That means the incumbent President of the country (also from the ANC, so far) may finish his or her term while the new party president and possible successor holds power in the party.

In December, the ANC suffered the misfortune of narrowly electing Cyril Ramaphosa of the Colonial faction as its president. But the newly elected NEC is slightly tilted toward the Look East faction led by Ramaphosa's opponent, Dr. Dlamini-Zuma, mentioned above. And the new Secretary General—a powerful position—is Ace Magashule, also of the Look East faction.

The national electoral conference also adopted the Look East faction's program of Radical Economic Transformation, which emphasizes free post-high school education for all qualifying poor and working class students, nationalizing the central bank to bring interest rates down, and enabling the government to ensure that the land is being used productively, with power to confiscate land without compensation. These objectives are in line with the ANC's historic program.

Ramaphosa's London-oriented backers—including the Oppenheimers, Ruperts, and Menells—have been in-

Nkosazana Dlamini-Zuma, Ramaphosa opponent.

sisting that he must help them to immediately oust President Jacob Zuma, who looks east, and put in one of their own as interim President for the remainder of Zuma's term. When that extraordinary step was taken against President Thabo Mbeki in 2008, it badly split the party, and would almost certainly split it again now, and in the process, deny the ANC a majority in the national presidential election in 2019. A truce between the factions, to forestall any such split, was still in place at the time of writing, but the NEC is expected to deliberate on what it wants Ramaphosa to do, when it meets on January 10. Will Zuma, or will Ramaphosa, give the State of the Nation Address on February 8? This is how it looks at ground level in South Africa.

We repeat: South Africa is an important arena in a worldwide fight between two systems—it's either the dying British empire of money, or China's offer to share the methods of its own dramatic economic success with the rest of the world for a win-win result. There is no way to understand what is going on in South Africa without recognizing it. Indeed, the inner councils of the City of London and its Wall Street sideshow have been aware, for at least three decades, that they are no longer able to rule South Africa, and more recently, that proposition has been true for Africa generally. But the British oligarchs cannot accept that *Africa* should rule Africa, because it would likely become a great power. When Dlamini-Zuma wrote her "Email from the Future" in 2014 while she was African Union Commission chairwoman, she described the Africa of 2063 as a great power. For the oligarchs, therefore, it were better if Africa and South Africa did not exist.

For this reason, the same financial empire that sought a South African bloodbath in 1990—prevented only by Nelson Mandela—has ever since been taking steps to degrade South Africa to ungovernability and chaos, while keeping some window dressing in place to conceal the intention. It aims to derail the efforts of President Jacob Zuma, Russian President Vladimir Putin, and China's President Xi Jinping, to make of South Africa the continent's leader in the fight for the New Economic Paradigm, the paradigm of which the BRICS nations are the leading force.

Let us be clear about the nature of imperialism. For the British empire and most empires, the *issue* has never been race, but rather power, domination (even while racism is used as a tool). Even before World War II, for example, the British imperial center had begun to think in terms of moving to a new model of domination, based not on white colonial administrators or white settler communities, but on financial and psychological operations to control black governments—the neocolonial model. Under that model, the empire could no longer tolerate a local white ruling caste—even of British stock—for example, in Kenya. The community of whites in Kenya had begun to be hostile to London in the 1920s, with dreams of forming a white nation independent of the empire, ruling over black Africans as they pleased. The same phenomenon emerged elsewhere in Africa. Developments during and after World War II also drove the British toward this new model.[1] In the case of Kenya, the British addressed this problem in the 1950s, in a double-play against the Kikuyu people of Kenya *and* the white settlers.[2]

The British imperial center has never wanted any nation-building in Africa, whether white or black, but it thought it could more easily control black governments. The Kenyan example illustrates how the British oligarchs play the local elites just as much as they play everyone else, and the local elites have usually been loyal, willing suckers.

---

1. Namely, U.S. President Franklin D. Roosevelt was planning to force the dismantling of all empires after the war and arm-twisted British Prime Minister Winston Churchill to sign on to the Four Freedoms, an implicitly anti-imperial manifesto; after the war, the British no longer had much need of the agricultural production of the settler communities; and black Africans who had fought for the Allies during the war were more politically aware and also expected greater freedom as recompense.

2. The British manufactured the terrorist "Emergency" from legitimate nationalist impulses in Kenya and brought the British army in to deal with it. Then, and only then, with British troops still present, the British government was able to impose on the whites a government led by London's choice, Jomo Kenyatta. British operations to move Rhodesia and South Africa to the neocolonial model were more complex.

Makings of a Powderkeg

Thus, in South Africa today, the British oligarchs' intention is to prevent nation-building through a range of means that converge on ungovernability. With British backing, the local elite—mostly white and entirely aligned with the policies and morals of the speculators of London and New York—starves South African industry, agriculture, and infrastructure of investment. It uses the excuse that the country cannot expect to attract investment when there is so much political instability—instability that this elite itself has kept at a boil. The British also encourage financial speculation, which diverts capital from productive investment. They are deliberately creating an explosive condition among the masses by retarding the development of the country.

It is obvious that the British are determined to prevent the construction of nuclear power plants. It is less well known that the local elite, in line with British policy prescriptions, have also held back investment needed in the two massive coal-fired power plant projects, Medupi and Kusile, and cover themselves by complaining about the government's cost and schedule overruns, to which they have just contributed.

The iron and steel complex in Limpopo—now at last being financed ($3.2 billion) and built by Shenzhen Hoi Mor Resources of China—was delayed for more than two-and-a-half years by misleading "expert" advice in South Africa that the market for iron and steel was too weak or too volatile. That advice came to the fore in the Autumn of 2014, *after* the African Union Executive Council had formally adopted plans for a continent-wide Africa Integrated High Speed Railway Network (AIHSRN) in June of that year and regional rail plans were in the air! The Addis Ababa-Djibouti line was already under construction, and financing for the Mombasa-Nairobi standard-gauge line had just been finalized in May! A vast need for steel was on the horizon.

The financial press in South Africa is now creating a negative image of projects financed by the New Development Bank of the BRICS, such as the Mzimvubu dam project in the Eastern Cape to provide irrigation for agriculture, and the Moloto road and rail corridor connecting the three provinces of Gauteng, Mpumalanga, and Limpopo.

The leader of the financial press, Peter Bruce, who is editor-in-chief of BDFM Publishers, wrote last November that the country should focus on "agriculture, mining, and tourism" as "growth sectors," not infrastructure, agriculture, and industry.

Credit: Xinhua/Chen Cheng
New standard gauge railway in Kenya between Mombasa and Nairobi.

Endemic financial speculation is another form of the system's destructive activity. The British financial system was at the heart of the 2001 conspiracy to run down the South African rand. Again in 2016-2017, the British empire is obvious among the banks implicated in the foreign exchange scandal known by the name of their chat room, "ZAR Domination." ZAR is the currency code for the South African rand. The implicated banks included Barclays, Standard Chartered Bank, JP Morgan, Citigroup, Investec Ltd, Standard New York Securities Inc., and BNP Paribas. That list is a good cross-section of the British financial empire across several countries.

The still ongoing collapse, or near collapse, of the South Africa-based Steinhoff International corporate empire, after giddy speculation, capital flight, and cooking of the books, is another kind of destruction wrought by the British financial empire. According to Magda Wierzycka, CEO at Sygnia Asset Management, "The serious question to ask is how so many active asset managers in South Africa missed this. ... they should have seen what was obvious from the beginning: that this was as close to a corporate-structured Ponzi scheme as one can get." She called the resulting losses to South African pension funds "huge."

Black millionaire Gayton McKenzie is just one of those who have recently noted the consequences. He observed, on December 14: "Black people live in squalor. Rats and broken sewerage pipes are common in most areas. Blacks are spectators of white wealth in South Africa. You must be mad if you think this will be tolerated forever ..."

However, this elite is determined to add (literally), racist insult to injury through its vicious language in the press it controls. The retarding of development is thus combined with mass psychological operations to produce a combined effect. It is aware of what it is doing.

As journalists go about their daily grind of assaulting the ANC and President Zuma, journalists such as Peter Bruce; Simon Lincoln Reader, *Business Day* columnist; and Richard Poplak, columnist for the *Daily Maverick*, among many others, set the pace with their hostile vituperations, not to mention the frequently vile, syndicated cartoons of Jonathan Shapiro ("Zapiro"). This spirit is often picked up on and amplified, in Internet readers' responses such as this one from a Business Day reader on December 30: "All these articles paint the ANC in a dirty Brown colour. ... This really makes him [Zuma] a very very disgusting and a special kind of excrement ....to call him a man would be insulting all men. Let us hope he gets what he deserves."

This is not an isolated example, but a daily feature of the mainstream media. The viciousness and hatred of the language appearing in articles and responses, even in the supposedly most high-brow news publications in South Africa, also legitimizes and reinforces the language of hatred that black people encounter in the street.

Mayor Mzwandile Masina of Ekurhuleni, as the opening speaker at the Chris Hani Memorial Lecture in Boksburg on April 10, 2017, said: "Being shown the middle finger everywhere by white people ... must come to an end.... the issue of nation building and social cohesion requires all of us, not these insults that you get from social media and you get called everything else ... we are not monkeys, we are people."

Apartheid may have been removed from the statute book, but the traditional British imperial attitude that also resonated so well with most Afrikaners has not been cleansed from the proud and self-entitled heart and mind.

You cannot say that the top dogs "know not what they do." The destruction is deliberate. Gayton McKenzie reports, in his new book discussed below, that billionaire Afrikaner Johann Rupert, speaking on behalf of the British empire, told cabinet minister Fikile Mbalula in early 2017:

> I want you to go and tell your president that I looked after Mandela. But if he fires [Finance Minister] Pravin Gordhan and [his Deputy] Mcebisi Jonas, I will destroy this economy. My friends and I will make it look worse than Zimbabwe.

But the threat communicated by Rupert was chiefly bluster: Rupert and the people he calls his friends have been doing their worst to destroy the economy for years, as we have shown. President Zuma was not deterred; he fired Gordhan and Jonas on March 30, 2017.

Beyond the ANC

Now consider what happens as a result of years of ceaseless, daily attacks on the ANC. Many thoughtful black South Africans, *whether or not they support the ANC or President Zuma*, begin to see themselves as the implicit target. The British-directed business elite—with help from some think tanks and academics, such as the Eddie Webster crowd at the University of the Witwatersrand and the University of Johannesburg—thought it could isolate and destroy the ANC by means of psychological warfare, but is now faced with resistance of unknown dimensions that goes *beyond* the ANC, a resistance that comes—consciously or unconsciously—from the worldwide presence of the New Economic Paradigm and the optimism that it brings.

This broader resistance showed itself in December in three notable instances—in an Anglican priest's reaction to the political Christmas "sermon" of the Anglican Archbishop of Cape Town; in a dissent of the Chief Justice of the Constitutional Court from a politicized judgment of that court; and in a blockbuster book by Gayton McKenzie, leader of the Patriotic Alliance party, exposing the murderous manipulations of the elite and defending President Zuma. The three cases have this in common, that none was of a kind that the

Credit: SABC

Chief Justice of the Constitutional Court, Mogoeng Mogoeng.

ANC could just order up.

Surprise: the Judge. South Africa's Constitutional Court made one more contribution to regime change on December 29, by ordering Parliament to establish criteria and procedures for the impeachment of a President. The decision responds to an application in September of the British-owned Economic Freedom Fighters and two lesser parties which seek to force President Zuma's impeachment. While the court's decision does not compel an impeachment proceeding against Zuma, it attempts to keep the regime change process moving forward.

Chief Justice Mogoeng Mogoeng, however, wrote a dissenting opinion expressing his "deep-seated agony and bafflement" over the judgment. During Judge Chris Jafta's reading of the judgment in court, while it was being televised, Mogoeng interrupted to ask that Jafta also read his dissenting opinion for the record. Mogoeng wrote that, on constitutional grounds, it cannot be said, "that the President has never been held accountable for the non-security upgrades at his Nkandla private residence. That position would be sustainable only if the constitutionally acceptable notion of holding him accountable for Nkandla were nothing short of his actual removal from office." The judgment was a "textbook case of judicial overreach," he said. There is no option of appeal, however.

Impeachment requires a two-thirds vote. A President removed in this fashion loses his government-supplied physical security.

Like other moves from the British-directed side over the past weeks, this judgment not only targets President Zuma, but attempts to break down the tactical truce between ANC factions in order to shatter the party.

Surprise: the Priest. In his Christmas Eve "sermon," the Archbishop of Cape Town, Thabo Cecil Makgoba, demanded that the new ANC president, Cyril Ramaphosa, force the immediate resignation of President Zuma, a move that would likewise end the ANC truce and could destroy the party. Archbishop Makgoba works closely with George Soros' organizations in South Africa.

However, Anglican priest Maieane Khaketla of the Cathedral of St. James and St. Mary in Maseru, the capital of neighboring Lesotho, spoke for many on Dec. 27 when he wrote, "I hung my head in shame and utter disgust." We expected to hear a sermon on the baby in the manger, he said, but the Archbishop talks about the alleged misdoings of President Zuma, while "there are numerous cases of corruption, fraud, and sexual abuse against bishops, which the Archbishop has conveniently ignored." He called on the Synod of Bishops to boot him out, or alternatively, the Archbishop could just resign and seek political office.

Surprise: the Millionaire. Just days before the ANC electoral conference in December, black millionaire Gayton McKenzie published a book supporting and effectively *protecting* President Zuma, titled *Kill Zuma by Any Means Necessary*, now available as an Amazon Kindle ebook. It identifies the world-historical importance of the BRICS and the crucial role of Zuma in it. He writes that "a new order will emerge, and South Africa's alignment with BRICS is a strategic manoeuvre that could shield South Africa in a way that we may find ourselves crediting Jacob Zuma's presidency with for generations to come."

While McKenzie admires Zuma, he left the ANC in 2013 and founded the Patriotic Alliance party.

McKenzie provides detailed information, not previously made public, about multiple attempts to kill President Zuma by poisoning and sabotage of the presidential airplane. In the case of one poisoning attempt, reported in *EIR* in our March 27, 2015 issue, Zuma was not properly diagnosed and treated until he got to Central Clinical Hospital near Moscow. Attempts were also made to poison David Mabuza and Willies Mchunu, the premiers of Mpumalanga and KwaZulu-Natal provinces, respectively, according to McKenzie. They, too, were only correctly diagnosed and treated when they reached the Central Clinical Hospital. Of these attempts, he writes, "Mabuza and Mchunu were also nearly made to pay the price for South Africa's membership of BRICS." McKenzie also exposes other high-level operations of the British against the ANC.

McKenzie reviews the history of the newly elected president of the ANC, Cyril Ramaphosa, as the willing agent of the British empire and its allied wealthy Afrikaner families—especially the Oppenheimers, Ruperts, and Menells. They installed Ramaphosa in 1982 as the first Secretary General of the National Union of Mineworkers—their own creation for managing black labor. Ramaphosa had a law degree, but has never worked a day in a mine. When the time came, in 1990, for negotiations between the Afrikaner government and the ANC, the ANC chose Thabo Mbeki and Jacob Zuma as their lead negotiators. But the same wealthy families orchestrated a dirty trick to get them replaced. Ramaphosa became the lead negotiator. These families made Ramaphosa a very rich man later in the 1990s. McKenzie wrote that if Ramaphosa were to be elected president of the ANC (as he now has been), it "will be the worst thing that could happen to this country, particularly for black people, but perhaps in the long-term view even more so for the white population."

McKenzie is not dredging up the events of a generation ago without cause. Important figures of the South African financial elite were on hand on November 13 to show their support when Ramaphosa unveiled his very

Credit: African News Network

ANN7's Sifiso Mahlangu (right) interviews author Gayton McKenzie.

vague "New Deal" program at an ANC colloquium in Soweto. Reportedly these captains of finance included, among others, Colin Coleman, the head of Goldman Sachs' Investment Banking Division for Sub-Saharan Africa; Investec CEO Stephen Koseff; and Johan Burger, CEO of FirstRand Bank, all names well known in London and New York.

Now that Ramaphosa has been elected, it is just possible that he could now choose to become the servant of a far more noble idea than that of imperial domination. The possibility should not be pre-emptively foreclosed. His sponsors want him to preside over the destruction of the ANC and the country while they retire to estates in the English countryside; but he may wish to be the president of a successful ANC and a lively and growing South Africa. If he forces President Zuma out, he will be the president of nothing but an impotent fragment of the ANC.

African News Network's Sifiso Mahlangu interviewed McKenzie at length on December 12, just before publication. He asked McKenzie why readers should believe the book. McKenzie answered, "I am speaking about people who ... can come out and sue me. People who can come out and say, 'No, that's not true, we have never been poisoned, we have never been in a Russian hospital.'" Since publication, the mainstream media have condemned the book as "fiction," while refusing to confront any of its content. But McKenzie's claims were confirmed January 4, when the newly elected ANC Secretary General, Ace Magashule, at the funeral of Sandile Msibi, a provincial political figure, said that poison was suspected in Msibi's death and that he and President Zuma had been about to fly Msibi to Russia when he died. Magashule, a strong proponent of BRICS, also confirmed that David Mabuza had been treated for poisoning in Russia.

The broadness of the resistance to regime change or "color revolution," shown in these instances, is coupled with another kind of victory.

Another Blow to Color Revolution

The British-steered press has been forced to admit that it promotes foreign interventions into South Africa to change its government. For the past six months, the South African press has sought to *legitimize and popularize the practice of "color revolution," by name.* Most recently, on Dec. 20, during a Radio 702 interview with Energy Minister (and former Minister of State Security) David Mahlobo, the interviewer praised the practice of color revolution, saying it benefitted people who were losing their freedom under dictatorial governments. But then he turned around and attempted to explain away accusations of color revolution as defensive moves against the supposedly legitimate protests of "civil society." He attempted to get Mahlobo to name foreign governments he thought were attempting color revolution in South Africa, but Mahlobo answered that the government knows who they are, but as a matter of intelligence tradecraft, does not name them.

Radio 702 and the other color revolutionaries were answered at a Dec. 27 Christmas party for senior citizens, organized by President Zuma in Nkandla, his home town, attended by 5,000 local people. ANC Women's League president Bathabile Dlamini told the crowd, "The most painful thing about what these people are saying, is that they are being used by western forces in a desperate attempt to shape our own policies."

South Africa Chairs the BRICS

The year just ended saw important steps forward on the African continent, including victories in Kenya and Zimbabwe against attempts to install governments hostile both to the BRICS and China's Belt and Road Initiative. And two important pilot projects toward modernizing Africa's rails were successfully completed—the rail line from Addis Ababa to Djibouti, and the line from Mombasa to Nairobi in Kenya that will grow into a much wider network. Both use standard gauge.

South Africa assumes the chairmanship of the BRICS this year. It will therefore host major conferences of the BRICS, including participation of Russian President Vladimir Putin and Chinese President Xi Jinping. These meetings will organize for the new paradigm of peace and development. The British and their Wall Street ally would like nothing better than to create maximum chaos in South Africa that would render that nation's leadership and perhaps even the conferences themselves impossible, or at least ineffective.

Knowledge of the evolving strategic picture is crucial for reaching the next victories. South Africans, know the strategic map! Join the struggle!

David Cherry is a member of the LaRouche movement in the United States. Ramasimong Phillip Tsokolibane is the leader of LaRouche South Africa, of which Mokete Meshack Maxongo is a member.

November 5, 2008

Kepler's Actual Discovery: Mathematics Is Not Science

by Lyndon H. LaRouche, Jr.

I am, as you know, an old man, but, do not worry about me on that account; for me, being old has sometimes had some very important advantages. These are advantages which include such benefits as knowing, as most leaders of society today do not, what correctable errors sent us down the wrong path of the habit-making of our society two generations or so ago. Such were the errors which caused the almighty mess our nations now seem to insist on becoming, or, even worse. This is a mess which only rare cases of the more experienced persons among us would be likely to understand today.

For example, some decades ago, I wrote, that poetry must supersede mathematics in science. Some readers, even among my close associates in scientific work during that time, were shocked by what I said, but, they failed to heed my warning; rather, at that time, most of the relevant persons, even among my political associates generally, often bungled their way ahead, rather than facing up to my challenge that they free themselves of their often misguided notions of competence.

That contaminating element of incompetence to which I refer as already extant then, was of a type which persisted even among broader circles of those leading scientists with whom I was more or less closely associated in shared advanced programs of that time. The error by most among them whom I had addressed on this matter then, persists as a crippling factor in what, unfortunately, passes for learned opinion, still today.

Therefore, the following is a story well worth telling here. It is fully as important for the grievously perilous times today, as then; and is certainly far much more so
today; because, as result of that element in our past, we are now living in the most perilous times of all recent history for our planet as a whole, today.

The Thesis:
"Es führt dies hinüber in das Gebiet einer andern Wissenschaft, in das Gebiet der Physik, welches wohl die Natur der heutigen Veranlassung [mathematics] **nicht zu betreten erlaubt."**[1]
> —Bernhard Riemann, closing sentence of
> 1854 ***Habilitation Dissertation***

For me, fifty years ago, the struggle involved in my first, very painstaking reading, and re-reading through the German of Bernhard Riemann's 1854 habilitation dissertation, was one of several such experiences in my life which have had the relatively most important, and persisting influences in shaping my world outlook, up to the present day. The only comparable, earlier experience in science, of the quality of empyreal joy of recognizing the intent of what I was reading on such an occasion, had been my first, adolescent encounters with some of the work of Gottfried Leibniz.

Then it was the closing sentence, itself, of that dissertation which delivered the crucial effect—an effect on me, as among doubtless some others, which I am fully persuaded that Riemann had intended in leaving that particular, very boldly courageous sentence to the

---

1. "This path leads out into the domain of another science, into the realm of physics, into which the nature of this present occasion [mathematics] forbids us to penetrate."

LaRouche's early discoveries in the work of Leibniz and Riemann led him to "the experience of knowing the meaning of Johannes Kepler's own discovery of the principle of universal gravitation." Shown: Kepler; the M81 Galaxy from a composite of NASA's Spitzer and Hubble Space telescopes and the Galaxy Evolution Explorer.

NASA-JPL

conclusion of his address on that occasion. Riemann had already recognized the danger to society in attempting, as the empiricists had presumed, to substitute mere mathematics for actual science. The specific effect which that concluding sentence had on me, was rooted in the fact that that was the necessary outcome of the same Riemann dissertation's two opening paragraphs. This configuration defined: a relationship between those two "bookends," the one at the outset, and the other in the close of that same composition, were the likenesses of the opening and close of a great play, in defining the meaning of what lay between them.

I urge the informed reader to recognize that crucial aspect of the whole matter, now.[2]

Since that experience, I have enjoyed a confrontation with similar qualities of discoveries of principle, but none of them as profound for me as these two most

fundamental discoveries from the work of Leibniz and Riemann. Even Kepler's uniquely original discovery of universal gravitation had less impact upon me, not because it lacked fundamental importance, but because I had, already, adopted the same principled conception of man's knowledge of the universe from Leibniz and Riemann, at the time I had first read Kepler's *The Harmonies* seriously, about what is now about three decades ago.

It should be recalled by any person familiar with what became, over decades, my customary argument on the subject of method, that on all relevant public occasions, I had always insisted on locating the reality of experienced knowledge in the process of generating a conception, rather than in what usually seemed to pass among others, for the simple "bottom line" on the relevant topic. Reality is not where one had been dumped by a trolley-car conductor at the end of a line; it lies within the process by means of which you, for example, might have discovered the meaning of that way which leads toward that destination.

Therefore, as I shall emphasize in this report, my experience with those discoveries taken from Leibniz and Riemann which I have referenced just above,

---

2. To re-experience the effect which I had on that occasion, read the two opening paragraphs of Riemann's dissertation, and then skip to the concluding sentence with which he ended. Then, after absorbing the impact of that, read what lay between. As in Classical drama, poetry, and Classical musical composition according to the principle of J.S. Bach, defining the space within which the development lies, defines the outcome of that which is developed within.

should warn us, that, in matters of science, in particular, we must look beyond not only the realm of mathematics, but, also, even the much higher realm of physical science as such. We must reach toward that concept of the very existence of the universe itself, on which our comprehension of the possibility of the existence of the uniqueness of that universe depends.

Such is the experience of knowing the meaning of Johannes Kepler's own uniquely original discovery of the principle of universal gravitation.

On account of similar experiences during the years before the crucial experience of my early-1953, initial settling of accounts with Riemann's habilitation dissertation, I had had experiences in other domains which were similar to that electrifying reading of Riemann. This experience with those other domains included certain encounters with the poetry of John Keats and Percy Bysshe Shelley which are, in fact, relevant to the notion associated with the referenced, concluding sentence of Riemann's dissertation.

Among such relevant other items was, most emphatically, such a grand experience as that of the concluding, fairly long paragraph of Shelley's *A Defence of Poetry*, in which Shelley had summed up, with the most elegantly poetic expression of profundity, his view respecting "the power of imparting and receiving the most profound and impassioned conceptions respecting man and nature." What Shelley wrote there, in the paragraph as a whole, corresponds to my entire retrospective and prospective view of the proper organization of our attempted insights into the dynamics of the social processes of human experience and development.

It was the convergence of my sense of things respecting both such fundamentals of physical science, and of great Classical poetry and drama such as that, which has defined the heart and mind of my conscience, from my adolescence, through today. For me, as I emphasize in the two chapters which follow these introductory remarks, this recurring, life-long experience of mine goes to the heart of what I am, personally, most passionately committed to convey to the benefit of coming generations, including the promise

EIRNS/Philip Ulanowsky

LaRouche shocked a group of scientists in the 1980s, by insisting that the problems of physics, "must be addressed by aid of attention to the details of Kepler's discovery of the principle of universal Solar gravitation." Only Dr. Robert Moon (shown here giving a science class) had a positive response.

of that which awaits them, emergent, as within some parts of the young adult generation of the present moment.

A Certain Crisis in Science

So, consequently, on the occasion of a meeting convened at Ibykus Farm back during the mid-1980s, I shocked the assembled scientists of our international Fusion Energy Foundation (FEF), by insisting that the problems of physics which were confronting us then, must be addressed by aid of attention to the details of Kepler's discovery of the principle of universal solar gravitation. I situated my argument to that effect, in the domain of my special competence as—as, in effect, already, then—a leading physical economist of the world today. Such was my tested competence in a Riemannian science of physical economy. Most among those assembled at that meeting had been enraged by my introduction of this as a matter of policy, excepting, from a somewhat older generation, Chicago's celebrated Professor Robert Moon.

That rage, from many at that table, expressed, es-

EIRNS/Eric Thomas

Above, a statue of Leonardo in Florence; his panoramic view of the Arno Valley.

Filippo Brunelleschi introduced the physical principle of the catenary function for crafting the cupola of the Cathedral of Florence, and Cusa follower Leonardo da Vinci revolutionized the notion of sight, preceding Kepler in challenging the superstition of sense-certainty, represented by Euclid's Elements.

Courtesy of Pennie Sabel

Filippo, above, looks up at his great dome; the interior of the cathedral; the inset shows a cutaway of interior structure.

sentially, a knee-jerk reaction to any attack on what had been presumed by them, academically and similarly, to have been the absolutely sacred utterances of the Black Magic specialist, Isaac Newton. For them, Newton was deemed almost sacred among true believers. The believers included many otherwise competent scientists of outstanding accomplishment, but, nonetheless, still victims of youthful classroom indoctrination in what had been built up into the form of a shabby cult-ritual around that dubious English creature.

In retrospect, looking back over the twenty-odd years since that particular FEF meeting, I had been completely correct in every feature of what I delivered, on the point of my argument then. The relevant evidence re-examined, repeatedly, in recent times, has shown my argument, then, to have been thoroughly sound.[3]

Notably, the rage expressed when the same matter came up again during two subsequent meetings of the FEF, although considerably lessened, showed evidence that a large part of the such errors spread among scientists at that time, and still today, are a reflection of the fact that the generation of scientists produced from among returning World War II veterans had studied virtually nothing of Kepler's actual work. Most among

____

3. As the argument against the Leibniz calculus from the Eighteenth-

Century empiricists, such as D'Alembert, Euler, and Lagrange, typifies the case, empiricism, in fact, permits no explicitly mathematical consideration of a universal physical principle's impact upon the process of society considered as a whole. As financial accounting and related aspects of economic practice illustrate the point, today's taught mathematics permits no efficient consideration of this role of universal physical principles. This has been a crippling feature in the attempt of many professionals to assess the impact of fundamental discoveries of physical principle on the increase of the physical productivity of investment of science on labor, infrastructure, and other matters of crucial importance. My argument was a proposal to address the principled implications of any science-driver program.

them knew almost nothing about the way in which the deepest issues of modern science, which had been posed, uniquely, by those kinds of discoveries typified by Kepler's own, had been fraudulently put aside during the centuries, put aside despite the *De Docta Ignorantia* of the actual, Fifteenth-Century founder of modern physical science, Cardinal Nicholas of Cusa.[4]

This same, inherently destructive error by my own critics, within FEF and elsewhere during the 1980s, and, again, now, lies in what they copied from the Newton cult's libels against Kepler. The influence of that same philosophically reductionist cult traced from Wenck, Zorzi (Giorgi), Fludd, and Sarpi's lackey Galileo, is a tradition which persists today, usually in a more vicious form today than that of the past. The folly of that cult is now a tradition which has been formed under the influence of the far greater decadence which has been recently accumulated in the dogmas and expositions among leading academic institutions. Such has been the effect, for science and science education today, which is to be recognized in the tattered condition of higher education today, since the passing away of most among the representatives of three adult generations of matured adults, including the two preceding my own.

Those have been three generations which had represented a certain quality of relative scientific competence which has been largely lost, or threatened with virtually total loss, today. These three past generations, whose existence as a group of three generations, is dated largely from about the beginning of the Twentieth Century, still represented a repository of some degree of "pre-68er" relative competence. Theirs was a competence, if sometimes a bit damaged epistemologically, which was relatively commonplace among professionals, still a generation ago, before the takeover of almost everything by the continuing, corrosive effects of the 1968 insurgency of the virtually Dionysian cult of the "post-industrial" age of "globalization."[5]

The most notable feature of the post-1968 process of accelerating moral and intellectual degeneration of modern academic and related institutions, had been its nature as a successor to and an outgrowth of the successive steps toward utter degeneracy in the teaching of science marked, at the close of the Nineteenth Century, by the decadent "mechanics" of the positivist Ernst Mach and his immediate followers, and, then, the numerologists' Twentieth-Century lunacy of the cult of Bertrand Russell, and of such among the devotees of Russell's sordid *Principia Mathematica* as Norbert Wiener and John von Neumann.

The spread of the existentialist, deconstructionist cult into its currently prevalent form of utter moral depravity, would not have been sustainable to this effect, had the natural forces of opposition to unreason not been corrupted in that way. Typically, that corruption is symptomized by the fact, that today's source of that incompetence which is illustrated, typically, by principal objections which have been employed against Kepler, is to be found in the intentionally justly derogatory implications of Friedrich Schiller's use of the term, *Brotgelehrten*. For example, for the generation of students entering universities during the terms of President Truman, or later, the intent to be awarded their degrees, and to secure advances into post-graduate employment, were frequently overriding concerns. "Truth?" "Yes, of course," they say, "whenever possible; but, you have to be practical, if you do not wish to risk your career." The sophistry of the high priesthood of Old Babylon was always the nastiest phase of that ancient society's successors.

That sort of corruption of the body of academic and related practice of physical sciences goes on, and on, and on, worse than ever, since then, today. Some of the worst has been encountered lately among the faculty at Harvard University; but, corruption of a similar quality is also pervasive in today's relevant institutions.[6]

So, whereas that sort of corruption already existed, in a milder form, among what were otherwise useful scientists twenty or more years ago, the prospects for competence in scientific practice today, under the corruption now represented by the acute mental disorder of

---

4. First, by John Wenck's *De Ignota Litteratura* (circa 1442-43), but, later, the modern attacks on Cusa's founding of modern physical science had come from a figure otherwise notorious as the Venetian marriage counselor to England's King Henry VIII, Francesco Zorzi (a.k.a. Francesco Giorgi). Zorzi played a leading part in breaking the peace of Europe among Spain, France, and England during that time. The third notable attack came from the circles of Paolo Sarpi. The modern attack on Cusa and the work of Kepler copies the attack from the followers of the circles of Paolo Sarpi, who founded modern empiricism based on the medieval irrationalist, William of Ockham.

5. The "birth" of that "68er" phenomenon is to be located in the cor-

relatives of the founding of the existentialist forms of moral and intellectual depravity associated with the London-steered founding of the radically existentialist (e.g., Dionysian) Congress for Cultural Freedom, under British direction, in Europe, and the launching of the existentialist depravity of Theodor Adorno and Hannah Arendt in the United States.

6. See LPAC website feature *Harvard Yard*, www.larouchepac.com.

the "68ers" pestilence of so-called "environmental-ism," are often catastrophic.

Among the older representatives, among even the same circles still associated with me today, the case is, that excepting the independent type of young adults of university age typified by those who have been engaged recently in programs such as my "basement" projects, there is virtually no sign of oncoming new waves of scientific competence in the matter of method as such, in the U.S.A. or western Europe today; the very worst, is to be found usually among the digitalized devotees of "information theory."[7]

As some would say, when reflecting on the state of the world economy today, "Kissing buttocks may yield academic honors and (temporarily) well-paid appoint-ments, but does not promote insight into times ahead."

In any clinical study of the direction and rate of de-generation of the teaching of physical science, for ex-ample, over the recent forty-odd years and longer, we can not overlook the shift from a productive economy, to a "post-industrial" state of general intellectual and moral rot of the minds and habits of physical-economic practice of what are considered the "best professionals" of our economy of the present time.

In Cusa's Time, and Ours

Thus, that decay among professionals which has become representative of prevalent opinion and prac-tice around the professionals of academia and kindred locations today, occurs as the pervasive decadence of the recently prevalent trend, downward, in our society's widely accepted standards of opinion. This downward trend is expressed by the view that there is no possibil-ity of rescuing civilization from a post-industrialist's recently accelerating rate of destruction of a civiliza-tion now nearing a terminal phase of disintegration. De-spite the issue which I had posed, during the mid-1980s, respecting an attempt to return to the founding, as by Kepler, of a competent comprehensive form of practice of modern physical science, there is apparently scant chance, today, for a resumption of civilized life on this planet, for generations yet to come.

---

7. The progress of systemic devolution in the evolution of modern Eu-ropean scientific method has proceeded from the original empiricism of Paolo Sarpi and the hoaxster Galileo, into the rise of mechanist hoaxes such as those associated with the positivist Ernst Mach, to the nadir of radical reductionism represented by the numerology of such followers of the virtually Satanic Bertrand Russell as Professor Norbert Wiener and John von Neumann.

However, while the foregoing is a true statement of the recent trend in the state of world affairs, I am not a pessimist. I am only warning, that unless we are suc-cessful in that economic reform which I am attempting on behalf of all humanity now, a planet-wide new dark age of humanity were virtually inevitable now.

We have had dark ages of civilization in the past, and there have been recoveries from them. The Fif-teenth-Century Renaissance associated with the A.D. 1439 Council of Florence and the work of Cardinal Nicholas of Cusa and his followers, is the most relevant example.

In the broader sense of the matter, all competent forms of modern physical science are typified by the case of that Filippo Brunelleschi who introduced the physical principle of the catenary function for crafting the cupola of the Florence Cathedral of Santa Maria del Fiore. It is typified, even far more significantly, by the contributions to fundamentals by the Cardinal Nicholas of Cusa whose *De Docta Ignorantia* launched all com-petent specification of method for modern physical sci-ence. Although Luca Pacioli and Pacioli's student Leonardo da Vinci continued the legacy of Cusa with some brilliant steps forward, a competent general prac-tice of modern physical science itself, is rooted in the methods employed by Cusa follower Johannes Kepler, as in the original discovery, as in the *Harmonies*, of the principle of universal gravitation around which the Solar System is organized.

The universality of Cusa's mind required an experi-mental discovery of some specific, universal physical principle to match the far-sighted outlook of that mind. The uniquely original discovery, by Johannes Kepler, of a universal principle of gravitation governing our Solar System, provided that successful experiment.

Against that historical background, Kepler's dis-covery of a general principle of gravitation, as in his *The Harmonies of the World*, has an exceptional sig-nificance today. It is a significance emphasized afresh by Albert Einstein's emphasis on the fact that all com-petent physical science today depends upon compre-hension of the specific act of genius by Kepler, on this account.

By contrast, the assertion that gravity was discov-ered by Isaac Newton, has been typical of not only the greatest frauds against science in modern history, but of the capacity for corruption and stupidity even among what are reputed to be the best educated personalities of our time.

That said, I will now yield to others among my young associates the honor they have earned for their elaborating afresh the case for Kepler's discovery, in detail. I have made the point respecting Kepler's work repeatedly over a period of decades. My young associates have made the point, independently, in their own work. My adopted task here, is to provide certain crucial remarks, pointing toward the seed-crystal of the relevant argument, *with emphasis on the specific argument respecting the root of science to be found, still today, in the Classical poetry of two adult generations earlier.*

In this location, below, I summarize the most crucial, and, also, the least understood, but most essential feature of Kepler's discovery of a principle of universal gravitation. I follow that part of my summary, by a related, relevant summary of the case proving the absurdity of the presumption of the existence of some categorical separation of physical science from competent expression of Classical artistic composition.

Considering my age, I complete this report, and thus leave it to younger generations of promising talent to transmit and to enrich, in improved detail, what we have achieved thus, on this twofold account, so far.

1. Kepler's Wars Against Venice

The essential key to the solution which led Kepler to his uniquely original discovery of a principle of that universal principle of gravitation underlying the organization of the Solar System as a whole, was his recognition of the elementary irony posed by the contradictory effects of, first, examining the organization of the Solar System from the standpoint of a quasi-Euclidean idea of vision, and, then, examining the same motion from the standpoint of the harmonically ordered composition (hearing) of the relationships-in-motion of the Solar System as a whole.[8]

The systemic incongruities of the two dominant modes of human sense-perception, sight and hearing, guided Kepler to discover the principle on which all competent modern science education, and also Classical modalities in modern art, depend: *the recognition that the mere mathematical portrayal provided by sense-perception, is, at its best, the mere shadow cast by those true scientific principles which lie, ontologically, outside the domain of that which could be known through the formalities of mere mathematics.*

What is truly most important for science today in Kepler's discovery of universal gravitation (within our Solar System) on this account, is the implications of posing the discovery, to ourselves, of the notion of our ability to understand the organization of both inorganic and living processes, such as the *non-digital* principle of human hearing, as this experience is associated with the function of counterpoint, as discovered, uniquely, by J.S. Bach, existing within the presently known bounds of our Solar System today.[9]

This discovery of a universal gravitation of the Solar System, by Kepler, demonstrated the systemic absurdity of all assumptions to the effect that the universe is organized according to the notions of simple sense-certainty. Kepler did that in the most profoundly comprehensive, and conclusive way. All competent approaches to matters of essential principle since that discovery by Kepler, depend upon locating the principle of reason which governs the universe *ontologically* in the human mind, such as the mind of Helen Keller, rather than the mere senses. That is what is reflected in the genius expressed in common by Max Planck and Albert Einstein, in their opposition to the frauds of the respective followers of bad Ernst Mach and far worse Bertrand Russell.

The essential point to be recognized in reading Kepler's uniquely marvelous stroke of genius in that discovery, lies in the fact that, for the first time in modern science, he, as a follower of Cusa and Leonardo da Vinci, and also Brunelleschi, had directly challenged that superstition, called sense-certainty, which had been the leading obstacle to the successful development of scientific method in European science, since the fraud of the root-method of **Euclid's Elements**. Euclid's is the same fraud spread otherwise as the notion of allegedly "self-evident" presumptions respecting the nature

---

8. Famously, e.g., the very idea of a "three-body paradox" in a Solar system viewed by Laplace et al., (a problem which does not exist for Kepler's Solar system) is a devastating proof that Laplace's method, and that of his associate, Cauchy, and such followers of Cauchy as Clausius and Grassmann in the theory of heat, is itself a fundamentally incompetent one.

9. This implies that the concept of the Solar system, as such, must be extended to incorporate the relationships commonly underlying the respectively inorganic, living, and human cognitive functions within that Solar system (and beyond). This is implicit in the view of a Kepler-Riemann universe by Albert Einstein, and also in the work of Max Planck, as Planck's work is antithetical to the Mach-Russell positivist perversions of the Platypus-like images of "Quantum mechanics,"—the case of the curious hybrid, Russell, called "the scientist who quacks."

All competent approaches to matters of essential principle, made possible by the discovery by Kepler of universal gravitation, depend upon locating the principle of reason which governs the universe ontologically in the human mind. This is reflected in the genius expressed by Max Planck (left) and Albert Einstein (right).

of the human powers of sense-perception, which has come to dominate the classroom in modern secondary and university education today, British neo-Ockhamite empiricism most notably. The point is, as Albert Einstein was to emphasize later: he challenged this matter in a truly universal way.

Kepler's attention was aimed at the paradoxical lack of systemic coincidence between two sensory aspects of the observed evidence which astronomy laid before him: *vision* and *hearing*.[10] It is fairly stated that both of these senses, like all aspects of human sense-perception, do not present us reality directly; rather, like all good scientific instruments, they present us with *evidence bearing upon what should have been our desire to be shown the existence of ontological paradoxes which the mind must then solve by aid of the tests conducted in the mode of suitable experimental methods.*

The result of Kepler's discovery to this effect, was to shift modern European science's concept of reality, once more, from the falsely assumed, "self-evident" reality of mere sense-perception, back to the higher domain of universal physical principles, the domain of actually efficient reality.

The first problem which Kepler had faced in his role as a follower of both the founder of modern European science, Nicholas of Cusa, and the relevance of the work of Cusa's outstanding follower among Kepler's own predecessors, Leonardo da Vinci, was to adopt a critical approach to the assessment of the role of those mere instruments of sense-perception which we know, in simple-minded terms, as sight and hearing. Leonardo da Vinci had revolutionized the notion of sight; Kepler was thus to be recognized as being a forerunner of the great Max Planck, in the implied development of the implications of the function of hearing (i.e., the harmonics of a Classically dynamical mode of physical space-time, including sub-atomic space-time, rather than "digital hearing" or linear "seeing").[11]

The evidence that neither sight, nor hearing, presents us with the real universe, impels us to shift our idea of reality to the higher domain, in which the notion of universal physical principles, rather than sense-perception as such, *is* recognized by the human individual mind as the location of the reality within which the human individual, his society, and the effect of his actions are actually located.

Science & Religious War

Although I have covered this in locations published earlier, we have the following.

The success of the founding of the modern sovereign nation-state had been accomplished, to a large degree, on the initiative of Nicholas of Cusa, as prior to, during and beyond the great ecumenical Council of Florence.[12] This success of the great ecumenical Council of Florence, prompted a reaction from the already resurgent, imperial power of that same Venice which had, earlier, brought the Fourteenth Century's "New

------

10. E.g, the absurdity of presuming that digital recordings could ever replicate actual music.

11. A relevant account of the work of Max Planck and his notable adversaries in science has been supplied recently by Caroline Hartmann for the occasion of Planck's 150th Birthday ("On Honesty towards Nature," Wiesbaden: *Neue Solidarität*, 18:2008). The frauds against Planck by, first, the followers of Ernst Mach, during the period of World War I, and the later frauds by the circles of Bertrand Russell, are a relevant subject for those wishing to follow up my discussion here. Classical dynamics, as introduced to modern science by Leibniz, in the 1690s, references the Pythagoreans and Plato, and anticipates Riemann, Max Planck, and Albert Einstein. On this account, the absurdity of such as Euclid, Claudius Ptolemy, the modern empiricists, and the pathological cases of the followers of Ernst Mach and Bertrand Russell, are implicitly referenced here.

12. *Concordancia Catholica*, *De Docta Ignorantia*, *De Pace Fidei*, et al.

Dark Age" upon Europe through aid of the Lombard League of the Fourteenth Century New Dark Age.

In the later half of the Fifteenth Century, the ancient evil of usurious Venice was then regaining much of the predatory, usurious, political power of its financier class. It was focusing that power strategically, politically, with the intention of breaking-up the unity of leading sections of western and eastern Christianity through the special operations against targets Moscow, the Balkans, and Constantinople. This led to the outbreak of a long period of religious warfare throughout Europe, from the launching of the expulsion of the Jews from Spain, in 1492, until the 1648 Peace of Westphalia.

The motive for the philosophical reductionists' systematic denial of the human individual's access to that reality of cause-effect which lies beyond the domain of mere sense-perception, was the intent of the rulers of society to make virtual slaves of their subjects, by denying those subjects access to *secure knowledge of those creative powers of the human individual mind which set the human species above all other species*. So, the denial of the knowledgeable use of "fire" by the Olympian Zeus of Aeschylus' ***Prometheus Bound***, degraded mortal human individuals, as the followers of Britain's Prince Philip and his lying lackey, former Vice-President Al Gore, do, into virtually mere cattle of the rulers of empires and their like.

There are two of today's representatives from among the tradition of the most notable Venetian scoundrels of the Sixteenth- and early Seventeenth-Centuries' pandemic of religious warfare, a certain Francesco Zorzi, the sometime marriage-counselor to England's Henry VIII, and, later, Paolo Sarpi, who have a very special historic significance, still today. This latter pair's strategic pranks against modern civilization, have been of crucial significance for understanding the roots of the types of problems which continue to afflict today's now globally-extended European civilization: the types of problems represented by the enslavement of mankind by the Olympian Zeus' prohibition of ordinary human individuals' access to useful knowledge of "fire."

The first relevant case of such would-be Olympian

Venetian superspy Francesco Zorzi promoted the marriage (in 1533) of the seductress Anne Boleyn, to the English King Henry VIII, as part of his campaign to divide Europe between warring Catholics and Protestants. The spread of religious warfare would continue until the 1648 Treaty of Westphalia. The portrait of Henry is by Hans Holbein the Younger.

ideological oppressors in modern European society, is typified by the case of the Venetian super-spy and bitter adversary of the work of Cardinal Nicholas of Cusa's founding of modern physical science, Francesco Zorzi (a.k.a. Giorgi). That was the Zorzi who was crucial in the work of organizing the general religious warfare among Catholics and Protestants, an effort he conducted through aid of his orchestration of the role of Venice's agents such as Cardinal Pole and Thomas Cromwell. The effects of this included the case of Anne Boleyn, the latter she who was used as a mere sexual plaything by Zorzi, in his special role as marriage-counselor to England's Henry VIII, in orchestrating the division of Europe between a Protestant North and a Catholic South. The turning of England in this way, was crucial in the perpetuation, and spread of the religious warfare which would not be ended until the signal intervention by Cardinal Mazarin into the process which became known as the 1648 Peace of Westphalia.

The second case, of more immediate importance than Zorzi for today's modern scientific and strategic controversies, is the Paolo Sarpi who is the true father of British imperialism and of the evil it has spread throughout the world, down to the present day.

Both of these odious creatures, Zorzi and Sarpi, played crucial contributing roles in the crafting of that corruption of European science and morals known as British (or, better said, "Brutish") imperialism and empiricism. On this account, Zorzi is notorious for the attack launched in his *De Harmonia Mundi* (A.D. 1525), which was his attack on Nicholas of Cusa's *De Docta Ignorantia*. (A.D. 1440). Zorzi's attack was conclusively rebutted for physical science, later, by Kepler, in Kepler's *Harmonies of the World*. The fresh attack, then, from Sarpi's version of irrationalism, is the most significant for history since the close of the Sixteenth Century.

The key to understanding the physically strategic significance of the difference between the modern Aristoteleans and Sarpi, is to be recognized in the effects of the unleashing of a limited degree of technological progress in social relations and productive powers of labor by Sarpi's followers, who thus attempted to catch up with some of the strategically significant technological advantages which had been the immediate result of the scientific revolution launched in Florence through the work of Brunelleschi, and, more emphatically, Nicholas of Cusa. The strategically crucial issue here, is the scientific and technological superiority of a culture rooted in science, over the sterility of both the Aristotelean tradition, and the surrogate for Aristoteleanism met in the mystical reductionism of the empiricist, positivist, and existentialist followers of Paolo Sarpi: *modern philosophical Liberalism*.

The Great Lie of Liberalism

Thus, until Sarpi's emergence as a leading power of his faction, in the wake of the Council of Trent, the most crucial strategic weakness of the Venice-directed campaigns of war against the modern nation-state, had been the crippling effect of the influence, on the Venetian cause, of the Aristotelean argument copied by the *a-priori* presumptions of Euclidean Geometry. This was the argument which had been crucial in blocking scientific-technological progress, and therefore strategic capabilities, among the so-called Catholic faction.

Sarpi's strategically crucial innovation was his evasion, if only in a relatively significant degree, of the self-inflicted problem of stagnation, inherent in Aristotle's doctrine; this is the relative weakness which Sarpi overcame partially, through a swindle, his resurrection of the teachings of a medieval irrationalist, William of Ockham (Latin: Occam).

Sarpi's adoption of Ockham's irrationalism allowed Sarpi's Venetian faction some latitude for the strategically significant, mechanistic application of technological progress, but, at the same time, relied on Ockham's principle of obscurantism to prevent the spread of knowledge of the actual scientific principles. This specific kind of irrationalism permeated Sarpi's adoption of Ockham; this form of systemic irrationalism became known as empiricism, or modern Anglo-Dutch Liberalism. So, Sarpi bent the law of anti-creativity associated with what Aeschylus had treated as the Olympian Zeus, but without actually violating that characteristic principle of ancient and modern Euro-Asiatic oligarchical systems.

The specific types of frauds which the followers of Sarpi employed for methods of suppression of knowledge of the discovery of actual principles of science, are typified by the Anglo-Dutch Liberal empiricist's fraudulent suppression of the evidence of Kepler's actual, uniquely original discovery of the principle of gravitation. Later, from the second half of the Nineteenth Century, more radically irrational forms of empiricism were adopted by the Liberals, as this was typified by the followers of the positivist Ernst Mach, and, then, Bertrand Russell. The claims for discovery of gravitation by Isaac Newton, are entirely a product of those deliberate, pagan, quasi-religious frauds of the empiricists, frauds presently dominant in many university science departments to the present day.

The more general outcome of the kinds of empiricist frauds spread by the followers of Sarpi in modern university programs, has been the substitution of mathematical formulas for actual discoveries of principle — *the substitution of shadow (the mathematical formulation) for substance (the crucial experimental experience)*. As in the case of Kepler's discovery of general gravitation in the Solar System, the actuality of the action of gravitation is expressed in terms of a quality of infinitesimal which is to be defined as ontological, rather than mathematical in nature.

Einstein's Truth

In opposition to the pagan religious fanaticism of reductionist cults in the tradition of Sarpi, the standard Twentieth Century argument for defining Kepler's unique originality in the matter of the historically actual discovery of Solar gravitation, is that which was made by Albert Einstein. I restate that case as I have identified it in earlier locations.

The great difficulty which had been introduced to weaken, intellectually, the astrogation-based science (e.g., *Sphaerics*) of the great ocean-going cultures which colonized the Mediterranean region's emergence, since about 17,000 B.C., from the long glaciation of the period, had been the turning away from the earlier discovery of great physical principles "enclosing" the dynamics of the stellar map, by, in effect, imposing a "land-lubber's" virtual "flat Earth" map in place of the stellar one of leading, ancient, ocean-going maritime cultures. The Sophist's imposition of the *a-priori* definitions, axioms, and postulates copied into Euclidean geometry, typifies this degeneration of science to levels below those of the *Sphaerics* of earlier, higher forms of maritime-inspired civilizations. Thus, instead of treating the universe as enclosed by great universal principles, as much of the idea of geometry as survived from the great mariners' science, was subjected, by aid of Euclid's a-priorism, to the crude sense-certainties of the local, brutish land-lubbering lout, or his incarnation as a modern British landlord.

The evidence of ancient known calendars, attests to the role of the containment of the visible universe by known quasi-spherical cycles of up to very long periods of tens of thousands of years, and even higher orders of magnitude.

Instead of proceeding from the stellar universe, downward to the locality, the Sophist pseudo-science had demanded that the Heavens submit to the dirt-bound view of the Heavens as an extension of the immediate horizon of the flat-Earthers' individual vision. Hence, the defective, *a-priori* presumptions of Euclidean geometry and the like.

From the considerations just so stated, a panorama of implications emerges for the thoughtful observer. Most important, the evidence of ancient calendars attests to the human mind's ability to adduce great principles of long span as enclosing the stellar system. This tells us something much more than the related evidence of modern astronomy. It shows us that the mind of the human individual has been capable, for as much as hundreds of thousands of years, in adducing great principles controlling our universe, "as if from the outside," that done through the agency of the cognitive powers of the individual member of the human species.

In other words, the ancient, medieval, or modern belief in Euclidean geometry's notorious *a-priori* "principles," is to be considered either as a hoax, or the outcome of a degeneration of human culture relative to what are for us today extremely ancient times—both options being pretty much the same thing, in effect.

This brings us back, directly to what Albert Einstein recognized as the authority of Kepler's uniquely original discovery of the principle of universal gravitation controlling the organization of our Solar System. It points directly to the absurdity of adopting the assumptions of a Euclidean geometry as the foundations of an empirical body of physical science.

What did the modern Einstein say about the unique discovery by Kepler, to this effect?

Einstein's argument assumes the form of pointing out that that infinitesimal of that Leibniz calculus, is not a *mathematical* infinitesimal, but, rather, an *ontological* one. The smallness of the infinitesimal of a Keplerian space seen by Leibniz's calculus, is as "small" as the inversion of the universal physical principle which it reflects. So, as Einstein demands, the universe as a whole is self-bounded by the set of universal physical principles of which it is composed.

The further conclusion is, that the universe is finite in this sense, although we can not presume that its evolution is *ontologically* finite in the larger, reductionists' sense of finiteness. We can not presume that the universe is not negentropically finite, rather than of a simply fixed finiteness. Hence, Einstein, in praising Kepler as the implied founder of modern Riemannian physical science, identified the universe as finite, but unbounded.

Helen Keller's Science

This brings our attention back to the ironical juxtaposition of sight and harmony, in Kepler's uniquely original discovery of a solar principle of harmonically ordered universal gravitation: a Solar System bounded, externally and internally so. The senses of sight and harmonics are employed, but neither "contains" the phenomenon of gravitation *ontologically*. Sight and harmonics are merely "instrument readings," but not, in themselves, ontologically, that whose effects they measure.

This is true for all our sense-perceptual experience, and the same notion extends to all of the instruments

Helen Keller, who lost both sight and hearing as a child, but went on to become a leading intellectual, epitomizes the principle that, "All really intelligent people are those who may be fairly described as creatures of sense-uncertainty."

which we synthesize for exploring the universe in the astronomically extremely large, or in the microphysically, subatomic small.

All really intelligent people in the practice of science are therefore those who may be fairly described as creatures of *sense-uncertainty*. We know the universe, not through sense-perception as such, but through appropriate experimental methods akin to those of ancient mariners adducing the efficiently ontological actuality of the demonstrable, measurable, so-called "universal" periods of the astronomical system.

To restate the most crucial point, we come to know the real universe as the outcome, for our mind, of the specific type of experiment which has universal authority in the same general sense as the ancient trans-oceanic mariners recognized the cycles which contained the universe within which they dwelled.

What we discover in that way—what we may rightly term "universal physical principles," or the like— become the means of our power to influence our universe creatively through knowing the universal principles which regulate its existence. Our power to exist, as a human species, distinct in essence from all forms of mere animal life, lies obviously in our willful assimilation of knowledge of the principles which are universal, in the sense that they, like the universal gravitation dis-

covered, uniquely, by Kepler, are the power provided to the knowing, to act in ways which change the behavior of the universe we inhabit.

So, the relevant LYM teams of researchers discovered the principles of physical science which I had defended, earlier, against many erring scientists, both in the Fusion Energy Foundation sessions, and in principle otherwise, as once more, here, today.

2. Poetry as Science

A conception which was subsequently proven to be very important, began for me back in 1947. I was strongly provoked by the effects of my reading of, and the consequent intensive debate within myself, concerning, the revised edition of William Empson's celebrated *Seven Types of Ambiguity*,[13] a book which I had purchased at a bookstore which I frequently visited off Boston's Copley Square. In the end, I was "provoked by" what would be the best description of that encounter with Empson which I might present to today's audiences. I came, thus, to recognize the indispensable role of the modes of Classical artistic composition in reaching a true insight into the most essential features of physical science.[14]

My reaction to that book of Empson's, had been shaped by my earlier, adolescent and later engagement with the works of Shakespeare, Keats, and Shelley. Still later, my understanding of the significance of the crucial role of Kepler's insight into solar harmonics, settled matters respecting the coherence of the principle of physical science with Classical artistic composition.

I had first become familiar with the work of these poets during my adolescence, from approximately the age of fourteen, onward; but, in the immediate postwar years, I read these afresh, and Empson, too, with increasing emphasis on that same modality, called Classical irony, which conductor Wilhelm Furtwängler sometimes described as reading (and performing)

---

13. Empson, William, *Seven Types of Ambiguity* (Harmondsworth: Peregrine/Penguin Books, 1961).

14. As in the composition of Classical music in the Bach, Mozart, Beethoven tradition, it is necessary to situate the subject within the universe, such as the phase-spatial universality of the specific setting within which all relevant development is contained, and with emphasis on the principled form of action of development which occurs as a process of transformation of that chosen domain.

from "between the notes." By "between the notes," I would suggest, as illustration, a comparison to the implications of experiencing a well-staged and directed performance of the situationally ironical opening quartet of Beethoven's *Fidelio*. This is truly Beethoven's mastery of the creative principle of irony in his expressed approach to composition. Without the irony of the juxtapositions of the mutual misunderstandings of the characters playing those parts, there could have been, technically, nice music, but, actually, no opera to have inspired the composition of *Fidelio* by Beethoven.

Important ideas reside not in the attributable literal intention of words and phrases, but in the irony which transports the mind's perception of the intended meaning to something which is not a deductive form of literal meaning. *Thus, the **New York Times'** comma-sparse style-book prompts the reader to proceed at highest speed without being obliged, by the author—or a keyboard artist, to pause for actually thinking.*

The combined effect of my adolescence's fascination with Classical works, and the excitement provoked in me by both discovering the principle of genius in Furtwängler's conducting,[15] and what prompted me, under conditions of my preceding, war-time experience, and my 1947 encounter with Empson's work, as a matter which prompted me to reopen for consideration: sparked a genuine revolution in fostering what became my rounded world outlook from that time, onwards.

In Classical Drama

All great individual minds have been the stages of a theater of the mind where the great dramas written by the spirit of Classical poetry could be performed. In most serious thinkers whom I have known well enough to recognize such distinctions, the outlook on reflections of both physical and social processes, has tended to develop in a way which unites the two kinds of subject-matters into an at least approximate, single, coherent world-outlook.

The best illustration of such connections is found in reflections on the principles to be recognized in thinking about the way the Classical stage, Classical artistic composition, and Classical poetry, inform what tends

toward becoming a deepening insight into all aspects of human individual and social mental life.

Notably, for our purposes here, all great Classical composition and performance of performing art opens with the presentation of a virtual statement of the global bounds of that in which a crucial germ of irony is presented as included. Take the example of the roles of Papa Rocco and Fidelio herself (Leonore) in the opening quartet of Beethoven's *Fidelio*. Another among the most magnificent examples of this principle, is the first part, *Wallenstein's Camp* of Schiller's *Wallenstein* trilogy, or the opening statement of a great Bach or Beethoven composition. An adequate comprehension of the working implications of what I have just stated here can be adduced by closer examination of these and kindred cases.

In drama situated in real history, which Schiller's fidelity as an historian illustrates, the principled notion of development is shown in such cases as *Don Carlos*, *Jeanne d'Arc*, and *Wallenstein.* The Classical historian-dramatist's intention is never the production of entertaining fiction, nor silly homilies in the alleged service of "morality." As I have emphasized the point for the case of the Homeric *Iliad*, the essence of all effective Classical drama, is to use the audience's powers of imagination to unmask the ghost which is the guise adopted by the corrosive principle of true tragedy. This is never the Romantic's silly idea of the "failed individual hero," but the systemic quality of moral failure of the society itself, a failure merely expressed by the doom which the society itself imposes upon that notable individual figure who does not cause the tragedy, but, rather, lacks that will, personal integrity, and insight which he, or she would have needed, to overturn the doom which his, or her submission to the society's own popular culture has demanded of the leader which it has preferred, and, thus, doomed, for that society's sake.

In the history of the U.S.A., for example, the recurring assault on our republic by the tragic principle, takes the principal form of ensuring, often successfully, that intellectually and morally failed persons will be brought in to occupy the Presidency itself. The miracle of the U.S. Constitution is that the republic has survived, so far, despite inherently failed Presidents such as, most conspicuously, Richard Nixon, Gerald Ford, Jimmy Carter, George H.W. Bush, and George W. Bush, Jr.

The power to resist such corruption as those Presidents, or nephew-of-the-Confederacy Theodore Roos-

---

15. A discovery which occurred during my brief, earlier sojourn in a replacement depot near Calcutta, in early 1946. My first hearing of an HMV pressing of Furtwängler's conducting—a Tchaikowsky symphon—changed my life-long insight into music on the spot.

The characters in Classical tragedy are induced to cause their society to doom itself by the influence upon them of the whisperings of conspiring gods and demi-gods, like the whispering Iago of Shakespeare's Othello *(shown here).*

Dionysus, prescribes the intended doom of those prospective leaders of society who resist submission to the imperative expressed, as against Prometheus, by the Olympian Zeus, or the Delphic priesthood of Apollo, or the Pythian priesthood's weird incantations. Such is the world of self-inflicted doom portrayed by the *Iliad* and of the Classical Greek tragedy generally. It is that culture itself, which is the systemic criminal of the tragedy.

The tragic figure in Classical drama, and in real life history, too, is not the individual, but the society which holds that individual brutally in its grip. The true hero, is he, or she who violates that popular custom which is, itself, the true villain, the virtual Iago, of that history. The intellectual *castrati* of society tend to breed defective children, and then wonder, "Why?"

Christianity, for Example

Hence, in authentic Christianity, it is the freeing of mankind to become mankind truly, through throwing out the devils which reign as do the gods in the *Iliad*, which is the spirit of man's experience of resurrection. So, what is most fairly identified today as "The Brutish Empire," is the singularly best example of pervasive expression of evil today.

So, this taken into account, what appears, if only in the opinion of the brutishly insensitive opinions of the ignorant members of the audience, to be the failed hero, is actually an imagined figure who is often all too typical of the pervasive moral failure permeating the institutions and population of that entire society. It is the, contrary, exceptional figure of great Classical drama, like the quality of leader represented by the exclusion of the legendary and real-life Cicero of Shakespeare's *Julius Caesar*, who is key to recognizing where the tragic fault lies—not within some mere leading figure, but within the systemic features of the society thus brought on stage. Hitler did not create Nazism; the British empire of such figures as the Bank of England's Montagu Norman brought forth Nazism out of the same British motives which had given continental Europe that Seven Years War which, in the end, had established the British East India Company of Lord Shelburne et al. as an Anglo-Dutch Liberal form of British Empire.

evelt, child-of-the-Ku Klux Klan Woodrow Wilson, the Calvin Coolidge who exhibited the prudence to shut up, Herbert Hoover, or the corrupt Andrew Jackson, Martin van Buren, or Polk, earlier, argues for the special virtue of a Constitution which is not a collection of do's and don't's, but a systemically thorough expression of a single, universal principle, as identified, most emphatically by the systemically anti-Locke Preamble of the Federal Constitution, a Preamble which represented a sacred devotion to defeating the great evil which dominated the world of that time, our great foe, then and now, the Paolo Sarpi heritage's "Brutish," Anglo-Dutch Liberal Empire.

The Principle of Tragedy

To state the case briefly, the root of tragedy is the element of systemic bestiality specific to certain human cultures. The brutalized mass, which has been subjected to the quality of reign which the beastly Olympian Zeus of Aeschylus' *Prometheus Bound* prescribes for mortal mankind, is the source of the depravities and threatened doom of entire cultures which submit to that notion of a beast-like, seeming changelessness of the principled characteristics of popular traditions.

In such a depraved society, tradition, as expressed by the Olympian Zeus or the Delphic cult of Apollo-

Nations and their people, in times of greatness, bring forth and select leaders from among them who are the essential instruments by which a people uplifts the spirit of the nation. Decadent nations perpetuate their own self-inflicted ruin by selecting mediocrities or worse as what are considered "more suitable" representatives of themselves. Such has been the essential, true internal history of our United States.

For example, in the Classical conception of tragedy in European culture since the Homeric *Iliad* and *Odyssey*, tragedy is typified by the way in which the whisperings of the Gods and demi-Gods, excepting the figure of Athena, typify the way in which the mortal folk among the figures on stage are induced to cause their society to doom itself by the influence upon them of the whisperings of those conspiring gods and demi-gods, like the whispering Iago of Shakespeare's *Othello*. It is the whispering gossips of popular culture and custom among the people, which induce the tragic outcome, just as a nation's majority may be induced to elect the President whose very nature, will mislead those who have chosen him, to their own doom.

For example, it is the clear fact of history, that it was the British who actually, intentionally created Adolf Hitler, as what founded the victory of Britain through that Seven Years War which had created the British Empire itself. Hitler was a disease, but it was the British system which created, and intentionally deployed that disease, as it, as represented lately by the Fabians of the lying Tony Blair government associated with the David Kelly case, have deployed my own and Africa's personal, typically lying, and mass-murderous Fabian and related enemies in the tradition of H.G. Wells and Bertrand Russell, still today.

In the crafting of the composition and performance of great Classical drama, the playwright creates a special universe, as, for example, Leonardo da Vinci creates space. In this space created on stage at the outset, the germ of an unfolding crisis is presented, as in the instance of Papa Rocco and the Leonore disguised as Fidelio. In good direction and performances, the lifting of the curtain shifts the attention of the audience's mind from figures on a stage, to the costumed spirits acting within a self-bounded universe, a universe of the imagination, bounded in a space and time all its own, but, as Percy Bysshe Shelley pointed out, in the likeness of the true spirit of actual history. Through the imaginations of the members of the audience, and the audience as a dynamic of its own, thus provoked, the development of the idea of true history, unfolds.

Thus, as Friedrich Schiller emphasized, the citizen enters the theater as an individual in his society, but leaves it a better citizen.

This is not fantasy, but the calling forth to the powers of the mind to see and feel the passions which move the souls of the phantoms on stage. The purpose of this device, is to guide the mere members of the everyday audience to see the real world of the mind in which they actually live, the world, usually unseen, but present, in which the fates of nations are decided.

In physical science, the same principle is illustrated by the role of dynamics, as dynamics was defined for physical science, most notably, by Gottfried Leibniz and Bernhard Riemann. A Classical drama, or the composing and performing of a qualified Classical musical composition's Bachian counterpoint, requires that element and its function within a coherently composed and performed composition which selects each ostensibly isolable element of the drama according a unifying concept of the development of the composition as a whole.

The celebrated "To be, or not to be," opens Hamlet's monologue as a dialogue within himself. The two elements of that opening define the characteristic motion of the entire drama of that soliloquy, and reflect the principle of all that which came before and will follow, *dynamically*. All great works for performance on the stage, or in other modes, must begin as does Part I of Friedrich Schiller's *Wallenstein* trilogy, with the global parameters within which the entire, unfolding remainder of the drama must express its unifying principle of unfolding development. If you do not see the evil of the true history which that trilogy expresses, you understood nothing of either the intention of Schiller as a leading historian of that time, or of the history whose essence that drama expresses.

Here, within that certain wholeness with which the entire composition presents itself on the stage of the audience's mind, lies the appropriateness of the subject of the unfolding development as a whole.

'In Defence' of Beautiful Souls

There are two works from Classical English poetry, one Keats' *Ode on a Grecian Urn*, and the other, Shelley's *In Defence of Poetry*, which have affected me

Keats' "Ode on a Grecian Urn," achieves "the quality of a perfectly ironical Classical poem."

most strongly since my adolescence.[16] The first, for its achievement of the quality of a perfectly ironical, Classical poem; the latter, especially its concluding long paragraph, peering into the mirror of my soul.

In all valid science and true Classical artistic composition and its performance, the quality of message which sets the product of human creativity apart from the beastly creature's emphasis on simple literal pointing, is what is called *Classical irony*.

Return, briefly, to the second leading point posed by

---

16. Sometimes, an autobiographical element is relevant. For this discussion, I reference the crucial fact, that about the time I was 13, my paternal grandmother bestowed upon me a complete set of the **Harvard Classics**. This represented a significant, if minor part of all of the comparable kinds of the sources accountable for my education during my adolescence. What proved important in this, was the way in which some of the items within that collection did more to provoke me to look elsewhere, than to shape my knowledge through reflections on the text itself: Kant, for example. Among these, Keats' poem I found a precious stroke of genius, and Shelley a large-sized philosophical mind, a mind which can not be adequately understood today without assimilating the ironies of his **In Defence of Poetry**, especially the long, concluding paragraph (in the **Harvard Classics** edition) of that work.

Percy Shelley in his **In Defence of Poetry**. Here, in that paragraph considered as a whole, Shelley has summarized the principle of dynamics, as intended by Leibniz, but as applied to the higher realm of social processes, the realm of the existence and role of mankind in the universe as a whole. Look at the complementary aspect of what Shelley adds to what I had referenced from the same paragraph earlier in this location, as follows:

"…The person in whom this power [to lead society to great advances in the human condition] resides, may often, as far as regards many portions of their nature, have little apparent correspondence with that spirit of good of which they are the ministers. But even whilst they deny and abjure, they are compelled to serve, that power which is seated on the throne of their own soul. It is impossible to read the compositions of the most celebrated writers of the present day without being startled with the electric life which burns within their words. They measure the circumference and sound the depths of human nature with a comprehensive and all-penetrating spirit, and they are themselves perhaps the most sincerely astonished at its manifestations; for it is less their spirit than the spirit of their age. Poets are the heirophants of an unapprehended inspiration; the mirrors of the gigantic shadows which futurity casts upon the present; the words which express what they understand not; the trumpets which sing to battle, and feel not what they inspire; the influence which is moved not, but moves…."

Sometimes, I think of the period of association of Goethe with Schiller; but, then, I think, at other times, of another side.

Here, in poetry, we sense the dynamic principle of all those discoveries which empower the individual to generate ideas of principle which move societies, and, the planets, too. Science moves planets. Classical artistic genius moves the individuals, who move the society, who will move the planets, then the stars, and then, perhaps, the galaxies, too.